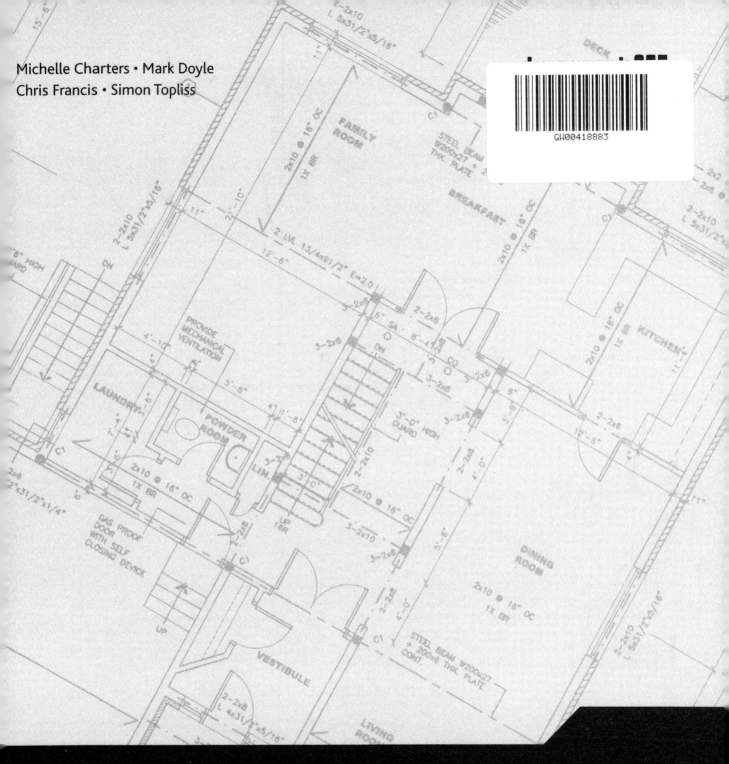

Michelle Charters • Mark Doyle
Chris Francis • Simon Topliss

Level 2 Higher Diploma

Construction and the Built Environment

Assessment and Delivery Resource

A PEARSON COMPANY

Published by Pearson Education Limited, a company incorporated in England and Wales, having its registered office at Edinburgh Gate, Harlow, Essex, CM20 2JE. Registered company number: 872828

www.edexceldiplomas.co.uk

Edexcel is a registered trademark of Edexcel Limited

Text © Pearson Education 2008

First published 2008

12 11 10 09 08
10 9 8 7 6 5 4 3 2 1

British Library Cataloguing in Publication Data
A catalogue record for this book is available from the British Library

ISBN 978 0 435 499 92 0

Edited by Sarah Christopher
Typeset by TechType
Original illustrations © Pearson Education 2008
Illustrated by TechType and HL Studios
Cover photo/illustration © Inspector © iStockphoto/Justin Horrocks; Blueprint © iStockphoto/Branko Miokovic; Building © iStockphoto/Yury Asotov; Tower © iStockphoto/knape; Dumper truck © iStockphoto/Trevor Fisher; Worker © iStockphoto/Hotizov Ivan
Printed in the UK by Ashford Colour Press Ltd, Gosport, Hampshire.

Websites
The websites used in this book were correct and up-to-date at the time of publication. It is essential for tutors to preview each website before using it in class so as to ensure that the URL is still accurate, relevant and appropriate. We suggest that tutors bookmark useful websites and consider enabling students to access them through the school/college intranet.

Acknowledgments
The publisher would like to thank Jan Emery for her valuable contribution to this resource.

The authors and publisher would like to thank the following organisations and individuals for their kind permission to reproduce photographs:

Page 25 – © Shutterstock/David Hughes
Page 45 – © iStockphoto/Chris Crafter
Page 63 – (top to bottom): © Alamy./Homer Sykes Archive; © Alamy/Education Photos; © Alamy/Pictorial Press; © Alamy/ARCAID; © Alamy/Derek Croucher; © Alamy/Edifice; © Alamy/ARCAID; © Alamy/Peter Evans; © Alamy/Education Photos
Page 138 – © Fotolia/Photobunny
Page 148 – cross cut saw © Dreamstime.com/Andrzej Tokarski; mitre square © Toolbank; all other tools © Pearson Education Ltd/Gareth Boden
Page 160 – all photos © Pearson Education Ltd/Gareth Boden

Contents

Introduction

Overview

Welcome to the Assessment and Delivery Resource (ADR) for the Level 2 Higher Diploma in Construction and the Built Environment. The aim of this resource is to help you plan and deliver this new qualification alongside the student book.

The Diploma in Construction and the Built Environment (CBE) is a composite qualification that offers a mix of practical skills development with theoretical and technical knowledge. It is part of the suite of Diplomas that are being developed in collaboration with employers to provide an alternative, more vocationally relevant provision for young people between the ages of 14–19.

The Diplomas will be available at three levels: Foundation (level 1), Higher (level 2) and Progression and Advanced (both level 3), and this ADR, together with the student book that accompanies it, has been written specifically for the Higher Level Diploma in Construction and the Built Environment.

The resource is organised into units matching the units of the Principal Learning of the Edexcel specification and includes the stand-alone Project qualification that also forms part of the Generic Learning element of the qualification.

The range of the Diploma is very broad as it has to cover all of the various sectors within the CBE industries. The Diploma offers learners an appreciation of the range of skills and knowledge needed for successful employment in the sector. Students will learn about and apply the three core themes that underpin the Construction and the Built Environment Diploma:

1. Design the built environment

2. Create the built environment

3. Value and use of the built environment.

This ADR is designed to complement the student book, containing extra activities, PowerPoint presentations and schemes of work mapping the student book and additional activities into sample lesson plans. With a requirement that 50 per cent of the Principal Learning is work related and relevant to the CBE sector, case studies are included to help the learner apply theories to real life contexts.

The CBE Diploma

The Construction and the Built Environment Diploma has been developed by the Diploma Development Partnership, led by six Sector Skills Councils (CITB ConstructionSkills, Summit Skills, Asset Skills, Energy & Utility Skills, Proskills and ECITB), employers and representatives from higher education and schools.

Building on elements from existing qualifications, the Diploma aims to meet the needs of employers by giving learners a wider appreciation of the Construction and Built Environment sector. Employers need to recruit people who not only have practical skills, but who are also confident with applying maths, English, computer and communication skills to the workplace. Other 'soft skills' (e.g. teamworking, problem solving and creative thinking) are all attributes employers look for in new recruits. The Diploma aims to address this by incorporating Functional Skills in English, maths and ICT, which are applied to the work context and developing learners Personal, Learning and Thinking Skills (PLTS).

The Diploma takes a holistic and integrated work-related approach to the built environment and Diploma delivery should reflect this. It will prepare young people for a range of occupations within the sector including construction, specialist building, building maintenance services, utilities services, facilities management, property and asset management and housing.

Learners will study the processes involved in designing, creating, maintaining and using the built environment, and this will include:

- skills and knowledge relating to the regulatory framework
- capturing and communicating design
- management and enterprise, including sustainability
- maths
- materials
- science
- management of built assets.

Key benefits of the Diploma

For Employers	For Learners	For HE Institutions
• Able to recruit young people who have a greater understanding of the CBE sector • Can be confident that Diploma holders can apply the key skills of maths, English and ICT to the work context • Young recruits have a greater understanding of the nature and breadth of the industry • Can reduce costs of recruitment and training	• Provides a blend of general education and applied learning • Offers an exciting, challenging and relevant programme giving learners a better understanding of career opportunities within the industry • Better prepares learners for entry into the marketplace • Combines the theoretical and practical skills needed by employers • Offers progression routes into further/higher education, work-based learning or to employment	• A good underpinning, academic knowledge • Development of PLTS and Functional Skills help better prepare learners for university

The Diploma has been designed to be delivered through local consortia of schools, colleges and/or work-based learning providers with employer involvement. This collaborative working presents a number of challenges for the institutions and teachers involved in both planning and operations management. It is important that consortia members have a clear and honest understanding of each institution's strengths and areas of expertise to build effective delivery plans and work closely together in a collaborative and fully coordinated way.

There are many different models of collaboration which can be adopted, but the two most common being learners moving to different institutions to cover topics where specialist resources may be required, or teachers moving between institutions. The model adopted will vary for each consortia based on existing collaborative provision, common (or lack of) timetabling, transportation arrangements and distance between institutions. The use of Managed Learning Environments across institutions can also help facilitate collaborative delivery.

Structure of the Diploma

The Diploma is a composite qualification made up from a number of components which can be grouped into three categories.

Principal Learning	The core content of the Diploma is sector related and focuses on developing the knowledge and skills that are relevant to the line of learning.
	A minimum of 50 per cent must involve the application of knowledge and skills to tasks, problems and situations that are related to work in the Construction and the Built Environment sector.
Generic Learning	Learners develop and apply the broad skills and knowledge necessary for learning, employment and personal development. Generic learning includes four components:
	1. Functional Skills in English, maths and information and communication technology (ICT)
	2. Personal, Learning and Thinking Skills (PLTS)
	3. work experience
	4. a project offering the chance to show potential and breadth and independence of learning.
Additional and Specialist Learning	Additional learning will provide greater breadth of study; specialist learning will provide greater depth of study. Those qualifications listed as specialist learning are related to the CBE Diploma employment sectors and support progression to further learning and/or employment in those sectors. There is currently a catalogue of 1211 qualifications included in the CBE Higher Diploma catalogue to select from. This list is updated quarterly and can be accessed from www.ndaq.org.uk

The Higher Diploma has been considered equivalent to approximately seven GCSEs at Grade A* to C, with an additional 0.5 GCSE for every Functional Skill achieved. For a learner to achieve the Diploma they must successfully achieve all the component parts of the programme of study. Higher Diplomas are graded A*, A, B, C or unclassified with the overall grade for the Diploma based only on the grades obtained from Principal Learning and the Project. Slightly different grade ranges apply for the Foundation and Advanced/progression

Each learner will receive a Diploma Transcript which outlines all the components studied as part of the Diploma programme. If a learner does not achieve one or more elements of the Diploma, they will still get recorded on the transcript and the learner will get credited with the appropriate Achievement and Attainment points, but they will not be awarded the full Diploma.

Principal Learning 420 Guided Learning Hours (GLH) (60 GLH per unit)	Generic Learning 200 GLH	Additional and Specialist Learning 180 GLH
Unit 1: Design the Built Environment: The Design Process (Internally Assessed) Unit 2: Design the Built Environment: Materials and Structures (Internally Assessed)	**Functional Skills** 80 GLH English Maths ICT	Selected from the catalogue published from the National Database of Accredited Qualifications www.ndaq.org.uk
Unit 3: Design the Built Environment: Applying Design Principles (Internally Assessed)	**Personal, Learning and Thinking Skills** 60 GLH Creative thinker Team worker Self manager Effective participator Reflective learner Independent enquirer	
Unit 4: Create the Built Environment: Structures (Externally Assessed) Unit 5: Create the Built Environment: Using Tools (Internally Assessed)		
Unit 6: Value and Use of the Built Environment: Communities (Internally Assessed)	**Project** 60 GLH	
Unit 7: Value and Use of the Built Environment: Facilities Management (Internally Assessed)	**Work Experience** 10 days	

Principal Learning
The key focus of the Principal Learning is to ensure that the learner's skill development is related to the CBE industry through the application of generic skills.

There are three key themes which run through the Principal Learning for all three levels of the Diploma: Design, Create and Value and Use the built environment. There are seven mandatory units for the Higher Level with 60 GLH allocated to each unit. With the exception of Unit 4, all the units are internally assessed and moderated. The learner is expected to produce an e-portfolio of evidence, which is then externally verified. Unit 4: Create the Built Environment: Structures is assessed by external examination.

It is important that teaching and learning draws on up-to-date developments from the sector, for example, the London 2012 Olympic Games, BAA Heathrow Terminal 5 and Wembley Stadium, as well as local projects.

With a minimum of 50 per cent applied to the workplace, Principal Learning may include:

- visits to employers/local sites of importance
- guest speakers from the sector
- realistic environments (e.g. workshops or on-site projects)
- case studies
- use of e-learning resources

It is important to note that Principal Learning equates to just over 50 per cent of the 800 GLH allocated to the full Diploma programme of study.

Generic Learning

In this component, learners develop and apply the broad skills and knowledge necessary for learning, personal development and employment. These are often known as 'transferable skills' or 'soft skills', which all employers look for.

The 200 GLH allocated to Generic Learning includes:

- 80 GLH for functional skills in English, maths and information and communication technology (ICT)
- 60 GLH for the development of personal, learning and thinking skills (PLTS)
- 10 days' work experience
- 60 GLH for the Project

Functional Skills

"Functional skills are those core elements of English, mathematics and ICT that provide the essential knowledge, skills and understanding that enable learners to operate confidently, effectively and independently in life and at work."

QCA October 2006

The table below illustrates the key skills which learners need to develop within the three Functional Skills of English, mathematics and ICT.

English	Mathematics	ICT
• Confident and capable with speaking, listening, reading and writing • Able to communicate effectively with a range of audiences • Able to explain information clearly in the most appropriate way, using ICT as and when appropriate to convey the message • Understand written information and instructions	• Use a range of mathematical concepts • Know how and when to use them (e.g. using percentages to calculate profit margins for a company) to solve problems • Develop analytical and reasoning skills • Be able to identify errors or inconsistencies • To use a range of tools, including ICT as appropriate	• Confident in the use of ICT tools appropriate for the task • Use ICT to research, select and bring together information from a range of sources • Use ICT to enhance their learning and the quality of their work

viii

There are a number of ways the Functional Skills can be delivered to learners: from delivered in isolation to the Principal Learning by specialist English, maths and ICT tutors, to being fully embedded within the Principal Learning by CBE subject specialists applying the concepts to the work context. Research has demonstrated that learners have more success with Functional Skills if they can apply them to a context which is interesting and relevant to them.

The Functional Skills will be assessed externally.

Personal, Learning and Thinking Skills (PLTS)

In addition to the Functional Skills, the PLTS are often cited by employers as skills they look for in prospective employees, and encompass the skills of team working, problem solving, the ability to meet deadlines, using initiative and self motivation.

There are six categories of PLTS.

Independent enquirer	Team worker
Learners process and evaluate information in their investigations, planning what to do and how to go about it. They take informed and well reasoned decisions, recognising that others have different beliefs and attitudes.	Learners work confidently with others, adapting to different contexts and taking responsibility for their own part. They listen to and take account of different views. They form collaborative relationships resolving issues to reach agreed outcomes.
Creative thinker	**Effective participator**
Learners think creatively by generating and exploring ideas, making original connections. They try different ways to tackle a problem, working with others to find imaginative solutions and outcomes that are of value.	Learners actively engage with issues that affect them and those around them. They play a full part in the life of their school, college, workplace or wider community by taking responsible action to bring improvements for others as well as themselves.
Self manager	**Reflective learner**
Learners organise themselves, showing personal responsibility, initiative, creativity and enterprise with a commitment to learning and self-improvement. They actively embrace change, responding positively to new priorities, coping with challenges and looking for opportunities.	Learners evaluate their strengths and limitations, setting themselves realistic goals with criteria for success. They monitor their own performance and progress, inviting feedback from others and making changes to further their learning.

With 60 GLH allocated to the development of PLTS, a simplistic approach would be to allocate 10 GLH to developing each PLTS. However, this time would be better spent in introducing and developing an understanding of the PLTS and how they can be used to best advantage by each student. It is important that centres delivering the Diploma make maximum use of the opportunities arising across all the elements of the Diploma, including the Principle Learning, for the development, monitoring and enhancement of PLTS.

Although the PLTS are not separately assessed Edexcel have mapping a 'baseline' level of learner engagement with the PLTS into their assessment requirements for the Principal Learning. There is a formal requirement for the recording of each student's engagement with PLTS and guidance on this is provided in the QCA document 'QCA guidelines on recording personal, learning and thinking skills in the Diploma' which is available on the QCA website.

The PLTS are assessed as part of the Principal Learning. What is key is that learners need to record their progress in these skills throughout the programme of study. So some form of initial assessment, review and summative assessment would need to be incorporated.

TOP TIP

Learners could use a blog or on-line journal to record their progress.

Project
The Level 2 Project is a stand-alone qualification and a mandatory component of the Diploma. The Project is an independent piece of work selected by the learner to help them develop their skills in independent enquiry, planning, research, analysis, presentation skills and the further development of their Functional Skills and PLTS.

The Level 2 Project offers learners the chance to develop their own learning experiences in an area of personal interest and can also be used to help them with their plans for further and higher education or career development. The learner needs to present a plan of their Project which needs to be approved by the tutor and awarding body.

The 60 GLH attributed to the Level 2 Project will be made up from a mixture of formal classroom learning of the underpinning skills, to directed/self study and one on one tutor support. The one on one support could involve tutors and/or employers for mentoring and support. This has an implication for resourcing and timetabling.

The Project is internally assessed and moderated. The Project is all about the project management process, not just the end result.

TOP TIP

If centres are offering a number of Diplomas in a range of subject lines, the project could be taught together using project management specialists or business teachers.

Work experience
This is the area which represents the greatest challenge for many schools. Learners have to undertake the equivalent of 10 days of appropriate work experience. The traditional approach has been for learners to be block-released for two weeks, when they spend their time making tea, photocopying and stuffing envelopes. Consortia will have to approach the 10 days' experience in a more flexible manner, working with employers to identify when they can accept placements, perhaps placing learners for a day, a week or for 10 weeks is more appropriate. The QCA (Qualifications and Curriculum Authority) and all awarding bodies are working towards allowing flexibility in how the 10 days can be covered.

One of the key concerns for CBE learners is that placements within construction are restricted due to employers' stringent health and safety issues. It is important that the full spectrum of the CBE sector is considered for placements, for example, council planning departments, council housing, housing associations, estate agents and facilities management organisations are all relevant organisations to approach.

If learners are to achieve maximum benefit from their work experience, tutors should identify opportunities to reflect and incorporate relevant materials and activities into their evidence portfolio. The work experience has to be recorded in a learning journal.

Additional and Specialist Learning
The Additional and Specialist Learning (ASL) is intended to broaden the experience of learners by including qualifications from other subject areas (e.g. an additional GCSE in French or history) or to allow learners to specialize by undertaking an additional qualification relevant to the CBE sector (e.g. BTEC First Certificate in Countryside and Environment or a health and safety in the workplace award). The Diploma Development Partnership is looking at the range of specialist learning and developing new specialist qualifications to support the Diplomas.

Centres must choose the qualifications from the ASL catalogue, listed on the National Database of Accredited Qualifications (NDAQ). The catalogue is updated quarterly, and can be accessed at www.ndaq.org.uk . Courses must be from either the same level of the Diploma, or one level higher.

TOP TIP

You can download the list of approved ASL courses as an Excel spreadsheet – much easier to analyse and identify your options.

In order to achieve the Higher Level Diploma, learners must achieve their Additional or Specialist Learning at Grade C or above. These would be assessed by the usual methods for the qualification selected.

Engaging with employers

Critical to the success of the Diploma is the involvement of employers. Not only do learners have to undertake 10 days of appropriate work experience, but 50 per cent of the Principal Learning has to be applied to the work context. The coordination of employer contact across the consortia is essential if employers are to commit their time and resources to supporting Diploma learners.

TOP TIP

Most schools/colleges have existing links with some employers. This information needs to be collated centrally across the consortia to risk employers being bombarded by requests from all consortia members.

TOP TIP

If schools have specialist status, they should be working closely with their company sponsors.

TOP TIP

Undertake an audit of companies the school works with as suppliers/governors/parents.

Employers can be involved in a number of ways to support Diploma learners:

- hosting visits by learners enabling them to gain an appreciation of their work context
- providing guest speakers to come into schools and colleges
- providing case study examples of previous work undertaken
- giving samples of products (building materials), plans, client briefs etc.
- allowing access to job descriptions and person specifications for employees
- delivering CV and interview skills training
- setting challenges for learners
- work placement
- work shadowing
- e-mentoring (particularly to support the Project)
- interviews or guest presentations which can be recorded and shared electronically across consortia institutions via video conferencing
- giving opportunities for learner Projects which benefit the learner and the organization
- 'Buddy' schemes where Diploma learners can link with apprentices or young employees.

Achievement of the Diploma

To achieve the Diploma, the learner must successfully meet the assessment criteria for all the components of the Diploma programme of study.

Learners will be issued with the following documentation:

- Certificate for Principal Learning
- three certificates for the Functional Skills
- a certificate for the Project
- Certificates for the Additional or Specialist Learning
- a transcript which outlines all the components studied including work experience and the PLTS
- an overarching certificate for the Diploma in Construction and the Built Environment.

If a learner does not achieve one element of the programme, although they will not achieve the full Diploma, they will still get full recognition and points for the work they have achieved.

Progression Routes

The Diplomas have been designed to allow seamless progression from the Higher to the Progression/Advanced Diploma in Construction and the Built Environment. At this stage, learners can then elect from one of four different pathways to focus their studies in areas of interest to them:

- Construction – the relationship between the built environment and the wider community
- Building Services Engineering – looking at electrical and mechanical engineering links
- Management of Built Assets – understanding the issues relating to sales, letting and management of buildings
- Management in the Built Environment – resource management within the industry.

However, learners could opt to take up an apprenticeship or enter into employment within the industry or decide to undertake a more traditional academic route and study A levels or the International Baccalaureate.

xii

1
Design the built environment: The design process

Unit overview

This unit asks the student to investigate the factors that have an affect on the design process for a structure or building. The student must appreciate the needs of the community during the design process as well as the social impact of any design. Full social inclusion must be obtained for all. The life cycle and life span of a project must also be carefully considered. Sustainability is a crucial factor in combating the affects of global warming and, as such, is an essential part of any design considerations. The student will investigate the carbon footprint of a design and the amount of energy it will consume during construction. Using good design practice to minimise the environmental impact of a building or structure is also carefully considered.

The student will also consider the impact of any proposed development on existing infrastructure, the local community and properties. The legislation associated with development will also be investigated, especially planning and building control regulations. The impact of planning decisions and the consequences of rejected decisions are also examined and investigated by the student.

The second topic area within this module investigates the utilities that service a building's energy and resource needs. The use of new sources of energy that can be integrated into the design is examined, focusing on reducing reliance on fossil fuels and the environmental impact of these new sources of energy. The utilities examined include water, gas, electricity and communications looking at their supply, identification and distribution. The national grid system is explored down to a local level to meet the needs of the end domestic and commercial user. This analysis should include provision for future service maintenance and access.

The final topic area explored is the ability of the student to be able to understand and apply technical information. The British Standards and technical indexes are investigated and examined with reference to their application in the development of a final design solution. This technical information is taken to a level where the building specification is revised to accommodate changing climates and weather extremes.

Links with other units

This unit links closely with the following units:

Level 1
- Unit 1: Design the built environment: Design influences
- Unit 2: Design the built environment: Applying design principles

Level 2
- Unit 3: Design the built environment: Applying design principles

Level 3
- Unit 1: Design the built environment: The design factors

Topics covered	Edexcel unit learning outcomes
The design stages and process	Know about factors that influence the design process
Building Services Integration	Understand how the nature and availability of utilities affect the design process
The specification for a building	Be able to understand and apply technical information.

How this unit will be assessed

Assessment is based on the student being able to demonstrate that they have met three areas of learning outcomes. These are:

LO 1.1 Know about factors that influence the design

LO 1.2 Understand how the nature and availability of utilities affect the design process

LO 1.3 Be able to understand and apply technical information

Marks are awarded across three banded levels with an increasing amount of evidence required to meet the higher band three outcomes. These are clearly specified in the assessment marking table within the specification.

Marks are awarded based upon the depth of knowledge a student demonstrates in each of the focus areas. This means they could theoretically achieve top marks in one assessment focus and a score of nil in another. Assessment foci are marked in three bands: band 1 generally asks the student to 'briefly describe' or 'evaluate', band 2 asks for 'descriptions', band 3 asks for 'explanation and justification'. Assessment should be based on a 'best fit' approach to the grid.

Suggested assessment

This unit is best assessed around a single project which includes the three main activities that meet the learning outcomes. This project should ideally be a live or local project. If this is not possible a scenario based tutor led project can be used.

The evidence must be presented using word processing packages. The student will be supplied with all the relevant information for this project namely:

- a description of the proposed project
- plans and elevations of the project
- a site layout drawing
- details of the main service provisions and entry points.

The student will act in the role of a technical advisor for a planning consultant. These deal with the issues around planning permission for the development, which has to be obtained from the local authority. The report that the student produces must focus on the following three key areas.

1. Describe a range of local factors and legislation that influence the design process.

2. Describe a range of environmental impacts as a result of utility distribution.

3. Evaluate information and produce a specification for the building envelope.

With each of these points the student should weave in the issues of sustainability and the impact of the proposed project on the local community and the environment. The evidence to meet these criteria should be in the form of an A4 word processed document, with each piece of paper clearly marked with the student's name and exam board number.

When teaching and assessing this unit, it will be easier for the student if assessment is broken into three tasks, which cover the outcomes.

Learning Outcome 1.1: Know about the factors that influence design

Students need to investigate the design process and the factors that can influence this outcome for a project.

What guidance will you give?

A real or historical project would be ideal to provide a wide source of information that the students can examine and analyse to establish the factors that influenced the design process on that particular contract. A guest designer invited into the classroom would be a valuable asset to stimulate learning.

What should you look for in marking?

The marking matrix is quite specific in what should be provided for this learning outcome across the three banded squares and reference should be made to this for the student's evidence.

What gains higher assessment marks?

The students need to justify the inclusion of sustainable design features within the intended project with full descriptions of these.

How could students present the evidence?

Information should be presented in the form of a written report.

Learning Outcome 1.2: Understand how the nature and availability of utilities affects the design process

Students need to briefly describe a range of environmental impacts caused by utilities distribution and briefly describe the key features of services distribution within the proposed project.

What guidance will you give?

The invitation of a building services engineer as a guest speaker or a technical person from one of the utilities division would be a valuable source of information that students could interview to obtain the relevant information.

What should you look for in marking?

The description must contain a range of impacts, with a minimum of three, and the key elements of services distribution on site must be described clearly.

What gains higher assessment marks?

In addition to the above there must be a wide range of environmental impacts described and there must be justification of the key features of the services distribution within the project.

How could students present the evidence?

Information should be presented in the form of a written report.

Learning Outcome 1.3: Be able to apply and understand technical information

The student needs to evaluate information and produce a specification for the external envelope of a building ensuring that evidence is supplied and that the design is suitable for local climate conditions.

What guidance will you give?

Technical aspects of roofs, walls, windows and doors need to be explored in detail to give the student an insight into the various materials that can be considered for this use in the external envelope in this specification. Reference to suppliers and manufacturers website would be useful in downloading information sheet on products.

What should you look for in marking?

That some, most or complete details required to make the envelope secure against the local climatic conditions have been included.

What gains higher assessment marks?

The student is required to justify all of the requirements of the external building envelope, providing clear evidence that the produced specification is suitable for the local climatic conditions.

How could students present the evidence?

Information should be presented in the form of a written report.

Delivering this unit

This unit is best delivered around either around a real design project or a scenario that will have to be constructed for the students. The assessment requires that they provide a set of evidence, based around the three learning outcomes, that the student has researched based on the real or scenario project. Access to a live project would focus the students onto a practical solution to design issues that affect the local environment.

The information in the student book for this unit is written in topics, each topic covering a particular learning outcome that relates to the awarding bodies specification. There are tasks at the end of each topic, some of which can be used to help with the production of the reports that have to be completed for this unit.

The activities in the ADR will reinforce students knowledge and can also be used to help build up evidence for the report.

Several of the activities are to reinforce knowledge learned in the student book and can be used to check understanding and be used as revision tools throughout this unit.

Integrating Functional Skills

Functional Skills can be applied throughout the topic both in the student book and the activities.

English – students will demonstrate their use of English throughout all the activities.

Speaking and listening – by contributing to discussions and making presentations and asking questions of outside speakers.

Reading – reading and understanding texts and using them to research and gather information.

Writing – communicating with others by using various written methods such as reports and letters.

ICT – students should be able to use ICT independently for a variety of tasks. They should be able to communicate and exchange information safely and responsibly, use the Internet for research and be able to present information in an effective and appropriate way such as producing text, images, tables, graphs and diagrams.

Personal, Learning and Thinking Skills

Some embedded uses of PLTS are incorporated in certain Edexcel assessment activities (see QCF unit summary inside the Edexcel unit specifications). However, use should be made of all opportunities to develop and enhance each students PLTS. Suitable opportunities will arise during the delivery and assessment activities for all of the elements of the Diploma. For example, the student may use their work experience to add to their PLTS experience and engagement. The development of the evidence portfolio on design will give the student the opportunity to use their personal and thinking skills in the solutions.

Linking to the Project

Some of the activities can be used as part of the students' project or can be the starting point towards gaining knowledge and information that will be developed should they wish to pursue this topic for their project. The relevant activities will point this out on the page.

Other useful resources

Work experience will further learning and understanding of how the sectors and services work together and these experiences will also aid work on the reports. In some circumstances this may be difficult to arrange therefore valuable insights can be obtained and primary evidence collected by inviting professionals in the sectors or services to visit and talk to the students as they can provide a stimulating input and enhance the learning of students.

Students should be encouraged to work in pairs or groups to gather information although they **must be aware** that they will need to produce an **individual report and project**.

Useful websites

- Your Local Authority planning Department link on their main website
- www.architecture.com/
- www.communities.gov.uk/planningandbuilding/buildingregulations/
- www.planningportal.gov.uk
- www.hse.gov.uk/construction/cdm.htm
- www.eais.net/greenbelt
- www.cfsd.org.uk
- www.sustainabledesignnet.org.uk
- www.nationalgrid.com
- www.StandardsUK.com
- www.canterbury.gov.uk/buildpage.php?id=1711

Insert Centre
Logo Here

Scheme of work

Title:

Centre Name:

Level 2 Diploma in Construction and the Built Environment

Unit 1 Design the built environment: The design process

Academic year: ....

Edexcel unit learning outcomes: Know about factors that influence design

Understand how the nature and availability of utilities affects the design process

Be able to understand and apply technical information

Tutor/Lecturer(s): ....

SB = Student Book

ADR = Assessment and Delivery Resource

Guided learning hours: 60 GLH (45+15)

GLH	Outcome/topic (SB)	Content	Student activity	Resources	Link to Learning objective
2	**Definition of the built environment and construction cycle**	• Introduction to construction and the built environment and the impact that buildings have upon it • What is the built environment and what are the local communities that are contained within it? • The construction cycle from the initial design and community consultations through the process of the RIBA plan of work	• Join whole-class discussion on what the built environment means. Mind-map what the term environment means • Whole-class discussion and tutor-led guidance on the construction cycle • Complete the construction cycle activity to arrange the cycle in the correct sequence • Suggested homework activity: Students to research the built environment where they live	• Activity 1 SB p5 • ADR Activities p16	LO 1.1/1

	Topic	Content	Resources	LO
3	**Town and Country Planning**	• Why is planning important? • The reasons for planning legislation • Greenbelt and planning policy • How planning affects development • What are the key planning stages for a simple building project? • What is a 'local plan'? • Why would a design be modified by the planning department before final approval?	• Starter activity: why carry out planning – students discuss issues in planning using a photograph of a developing city as stimulus • Drawing a plan view of the area surrounding your house showing where the different developments areas are • Researching and writing a list of documents needed for a planning application • Researching planning permission and possible objections	• Starter activity SB p14 • Activities 1, 2, 3 SB p15 • ADR Activities p21	LO 1.1/1
3	**Building Regulations and Control**	• How the Building Regulations came into being • What essential functions of a building do the Building Regulations cover? • The extremes of climate and the application of the building regulations • What are robust Building Regulations specification details?	• Discussion on the prevention of the great fire of London 1666 – students to consider how regulations may have changed this event • Web-based research on the structural part of the Regulations and their history • Identifying items that a building inspector would inspect a new build for, and equipment used • Documentation given for a development • Discussion in groups or pairs of the influence and powers of an inspector under the regulations, using case studies from SB and ADR	• Starter activity SB p16 • Functional skills activity SB p17 • Case study SB p17 • Activities 1, 2, 3 SB p17 • ADR activities p22–3	LO 1.1/1
3	**Community consultations and sustainability issues**	• The importance of consultation with the local community in any development • Typical concerns of any local community • Typical environmental concerns of any local community • Local community objections and protests	• Make a list of concerns you might have if a development were to be built near you • Discussion or individual work on concerns that could be reduced by good design and effective site management • Discuss which of the above are long-term concerns and which are short-term concerns • Use case study as stimulus for debate on how community concerns to be addressed	• Activities 1, 2, 3, 4 SB p19 • Personal, Learning and Thinking skills activity, p19 • ADR activities p24	LO 1.1
3	**Assessment Sessions**	• Students undertake the first session of assessment	• Learning Objective LO1.1/1	• Assessment portfolio/assignment task sheet	LO 1.1

	Topic	Content	Resources	LO
3.5	**Factors influencing design and development 1**	• Factors and legislation influencing design and development processes • Sustainable development and zero carbon emissions • Energy conservation e.g. embedded energy • Infrastructure capacity and availability • Building regulations and Town & Country Planning Legislation • Green belt planning policy • The needs of the local community	• Discussion on why decisions on buildings are taken, based around a certain type of building, e.g.: Where would be a good place to build a factory? What would make a location a bad one • Suggested homework activity: research government grants and schemes in your local area • Identify a local green site and establish what local factors would affect development	• Activities 1, 2 SB p9 • ADR Activities p18	LO1.1/1
3.5	**Factors influencing design and development 2**	• The importance of good sustainable design practice and examples • Brownfield and greenfield site use • Fashion and technical advances • The availability of land • Floodplain development • The effect development has on the local communities and their properties • How to minimise the environmental impact of a development	• Whole class discussion – what does the term 'sustainability' mean? • Discuss advantages and disadvantages of brownfield and greenfield sites; compare pictures and justify using greenfield vs brownfield sites • Prepare presentation on the importance of sustainability in planning a building • Prepare a presentation on grants and support schemes for building	• Activities 1, 2, 3 SB p11 • Personal, learning and thinking skills p11 • PowerPoint 4 • ADR activities p19	LO1.1/1
3	**Assessment Sessions**	• Students undertake the second session of assessment	• Learning Objective LO1.1/1	• Assessment portfolio/assignment task sheet	LOI 1.1
3	**Sustainable site practice 1 – community issues**	• The advantages of community liaison in any development • Reducing the impact of a project during construction on the local community • Involving the local community in the development • Understanding of considerate constructors and the added value scheme	• Starter activity: think of how the site management team could minimise the impact of construction operations on the local community • Visit the Considerate Contractors Scheme's website to learn about considerate practices. Discuss or prepare a report/presentation on how considerate practices have affected the construction industry	• Starter activity SB p18 • Activity 1 SB p19 • Access to computer and website www.ccscheme.org.uk	LO 1.1/2

#	Topic	Content	Teaching activities	Resources	LO
3.5	**Sustainable site practice 2 – environmental issues**	• The use of environmental good practice and its advantages • Minimising the impact of construction on the natural environment • What is embodied energy? • What is embedded energy? • The use of energy saving methods • The zero carbon home?	• Starter activity: discuss the impact of global warming on future generations • Look at a construction site in your local area. Make a list of good sustainable site practice that you can identify. Identify practice that protects the natural environment • List some methods of minimising waste • List energy saving methods	• Activity 1, 2, 3, 4 SB p19	LO 1.1/2
3.5	**Sustainable site practice 2 – environmental issues**	• Reducing a projects carbon footprint • Examples of low carbon homes • Examples of good sustainable practice in construction to reduce the environmental impact e.g. swales • The disposal of waste from construction • Recycling and reusing on a construction site	• Discussion of project outline • Study drawings and plans • Make notes on key points of project	• Proposal outline • Plans for development • Site layout drawings	LO 1.1/2
3	**The infrastructure**	• Types of infrastructure • How infrastructure availability and capacity has a major effect on development and design decisions • How current and planned infrastructure affects development/design decisions that are required for future projects • Be aware of the need to check the capacity of the infrastructure and the effect development has on community and properties in the locality	• Join discussion on what infrastructure is – lead group discussion on infrastructure in everyday lives • Take part in role play: where would you build? Use case study as an stimulus for discussion, based around a type of infrastructure • Work on case study – how infrastructure can affect design decisions, Discuss and prepare written report • Suggested homework activity: student to research the infrastructure around them • What happens when a utilities capacity is reached? • What are the alternatives to increasing capacity using sustainable design?	• Activity 1, 2, 3 SB p7 • PowerPoint 2 • ADR Activities p17	LO 1.2/1

Duration	Topic	Content	Teaching activities	Resources	LO
3	**The impact of infrastructure and utility provision upon development**	• What's the first thing to consider before starting a development? • The different types of utilities: gas, water, electricity, drainage and telephones • Colour coding of service ducts and pipes • The supply and distribution of services • Why is good planning of services infrastructure important? • The future energy needs of a home and infrastructure capacity	• Discussion – what needs to be in place before a development of buildings can take place? • How has infrastructure changed over time? What are the key demands on a current local project? • Discuss why a drain is not designed to flow when full. Research into other safe guards built into utilities to prevent accidents. • Group discussion on the case study • Investigate infrastructure issues in new developments	• Starter activity SB p12 • Functional skills activities SB p13 • Case study, SB p13 • Activities 1, 2, 3 SB p13 • ADR activities p20	LO 1.2/1
3	**Assessment Sessions**	• Students undertake the third session of assessment	• Learning Objective LO 1.2/1	• Assessment portfolio/assignment task sheet	LO 1.2/1
3	**Technical information used by the designer**	• Construction specifications • The importance of British Standards and codes of practice • Product libraries • Local authority guidelines • Other sources of information	• Discussion on why there are standards and rules for building and how these are used in a practical setting • Discuss why standards are used, and what benefits do they bring to the industry. • Research in pairs into further British standards codes • Working in groups, test a range of materials for technical information	• Activities 1, 2, 3 SB p21 • ADR activities, p25	LO 1.3/1
2	**Technical information sources**	• The role of British Standards • The RIBA product selector • Technical indexes on line • The NBS National Building Specification	• Students to discuss in advance what information and material they might need before beginning topic • Students to research the information concerning a particular type of material • Web based activity to visit the technical indexes websites Q and A sheet to complete	• Activities, SB p23	LO 1.3/1
3	**Assessment Sessions**	• Students undertake the fourth session of assessment	• Learning Objective LO 1.2 & 3	• Assessment portfolio/assignment task sheet	LO 1.2 & 3
2	**The Superstructure**	• Background knowledge to establish the specification for the external envelop of the building set within the assessment task	• Students research the building envelope and select their choice of materials in order to provide a detailed specification for the criteria	• Building drawings and details	LO 1.3

10

2	**Generic knowledge**	Report writing skills developed so the students can assembled the last learning outcome within the assessment	• Discuss methods of report writing, supplying examples for students • Students focus on the structure of reports – what is their format? What do they contain? • Students to practice preparing short reports, looking at how to present the information in the clearest and most eligible way. Discuss what effects bad presentation skills have on a reports reception.	• Examples of reports structure	LO 1.3
3	**Assessment Sessions**	• Students undertake the fifth session of assessment	• Learning Objective LO 1.3	• Assessment portfolio/assignment task sheet	LO 1.3
2	**Final session**	• The marking feedback and corrections required to meet criteria	• Students undertake any corrective action to the final report	• Student portfolios	All LO's

Level 2 Diploma in Construction and the Built Environment

Lesson Plan 1

Unit 1: Design the built environment: The design process – factors influencing design and development

Centre name: Tutor/Lecturer(s):

Aims & objectives

- To consider the factors that influence design and development

SB = Student Book 1

ADR = Assessment and Delivery Resource

Learning objectives

- All students should understand what influences the design of a building LO 1.1/1

Timings reflect one typical session within the GLH block of 3 hours allocated in the SOW

Total lesson time: 90 minutes

Timing/ Content	Teacher activity	Student activity	Resources	Individualised activity/differentiation	Personal learning and thinking skills	Functional skills
5 mins Welcome students and register	Check health and safety of the room Take a register	Enter room in accordance with normal procedures and settle quickly	Register			
10 mins Starter activity	Why are buildings positioned where they are? Discuss and encourage the class to feed back	Why is the school or college you go to positioned where it is?	Starter activity SB p8	Prompt students with questions if needed	Effective participators – able to join in discussion and communicate ideas Team workers – able to manage input from others in group and encourage discussion	

Time						
10 mins	Lead discussion on influences	Take notes in order to answer later activities	Influences SB p8–9	Offer note-taking grids to those who want them		Basic note taking to increase English skills

5 mins	Introduce activities, functional skills and ADR	Observation of activities in SB	Activity 1 SB p9
			Activity 2 SB p9
			ADR p19 – local government funding
			   – investigation into terms
			   – sustainability
					Effective participants – can discuss issues with others they may not know so well	Setting out points to explain to local people regarding the need to protect land

25 mins	Teacher guidance where appropriate – intervention by tutor to assist with students finding the activities difficult	Complete activities and ADR	As above	Make writing frames available Note-taking grids Differentiation by outcome – if individual student is finding it too difficult, assist with advice or prompting questions	Effective participants – can consider roles and have ability to debate, argue, give views and reason	English – report writing ICT – research-based activities
30 mins	Organise class to allow feedback, so students can deliver their presentation (organisation is dependent on the method of presentation chosen by the student)	Feedback to class on answers and presentation of findings from ADR activity	Computer Internet access Projector			ICT can be used during the presentation
5 mins Plenary	Review learning objectives	Q&A session to reflect on learning	What factors affect the design and development of a building? What must the construction industry consider carefully when planning any type of build?		Reflective students – consider what they have learnt to secure learning	

Level 2 Diploma in Construction and the Built Environment

Lesson Plan 2

Unit 1 Design the built environment: The design process – infrastructure

Centre name: **Tutor/lecturer(s):**

Aims & objectives

- To consider what infrastructure is
- To identify different types of infrastructure

SB = Student Book

ADR = Assessment and Delivery Resource

Total lesson time: 90 minutes

Learning objectives

- All students should understand what is meant by infrastructure LO 1.2/1
- Most should be able to identify a wide range of types of infrastructure LO 1.2/1
- Some may be able to debate how infrastructure affects a type of development LO 1.2/1

Timings reflect one typical session within the GLH block of 3 hours allocated in the SOW

Timing/ Content	Teacher activity	Student activity	Resources	Individualised activity/differentiation	Personal learning and thinking skills	Functional skills
5 mins Welcome students and register	Check health and safety of the room Take a register	Enter room in accordance with normal procedures and settle quickly	Register			

Time/Section	Topic	Activity	Resources	PLTS	Functional skills
10 mins Starter activity	How did you get here? (Starter activity SB p6)	In pairs, make a quick list of all the things you did this morning – cleaned teeth, made a cup of tea and toast, got in car, travelled to school or college, etc. Mind map this information in relation to using things such as water, electricity, roads, transport. Discuss who used what and what infrastructure it relied on	Paper and pens Starter activity SB p6	The discussion on what infrastructure has been used can allow students to decide what infrastructure is Feedback process enables students to share ideas Effective participators – able to join in discussion and communicate ideas Team workers – able to manage input from others in group and encourage discussion	Discussion and debate between students can increase English skills
10 mins Infrastructure	Explain the term infrastructure	Refer to diagram in SB p7, note-taking (using grids)	Note-taking grids SB p7	Direction for weaker students to use note-taking grids or mind mapping to organise their notes	
15 mins	Case study on infrastructure	How infrastructure can affect design decisions – discussion in groups of factors affecting design decisions Refer to case study SB p7	Case study SB p7	Allocation of groups to ensure good mix of students Feedback process means students have to argue reasons for their decisions Effective participators – can discuss issues with others they may not know so well	
15 mins	Where would you build?	Role play on where you would build	Activities from SB p7	Give guidance on roles of particular students. Those with more confidence to organise discussion; less confident to work with others creating safe environment for voicing opinions Effective participators – can consider roles and gain ability to debate, argue views and reason	
20 mins	Assistance on report writing	Write up findings from the discussion in the form of a report Review some sample reports	Case study SB p7 Activities SB p7 Sample reports	Writing frames provided for weaker students	English skills developed through report writing
10 mins Textbook activity and extension		Complete SB p7 Activity 3 and ADR activities (missing words and gaps activity)	Activity 3 SB p7 ADR p17	Embedding knowledge for all students	Use of IT in report writing can increase familiarity with search engines
5 mins Plenary	Review of learning objectives	Q&A session to reflect on learning	What are the different types of infrastructure? What factors do we have to consider when planning a build with regard to infrastructure?	Reflective students – consider what they have learnt to secure learning	

1.1   Definition of the built environment

Student Book
pp 4–5

1   Work with a partner to discuss what the word environment means to you. Record your thoughts in a mind map like the one below.

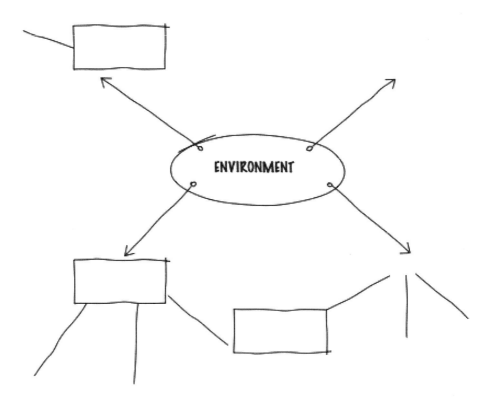

2   Look up the words 'environment' and 'building' in any reference books you have available or on any online sources you know of. How do these definitions differ? Do they match with your mind map? If necessary, add extra boxes to your mind map.

1.2   Infrastructure

Student Book
pp 6–7

1   Fill in the missing words.

The term 'infrastructure' refers to a whole range of basic services which society _____ on in order to _____ properly. Infrastructure means the basic services required for a _____ to take place. If you think about _____ a house or a residential development, there are many of these types of _____ that need to be in place before the build can start. If there is no _____ to services infrastructure, this has to be addressed. The _____ and _____ of infrastructure also have an impact on the _____ to build, as providing infrastructure from scratch can be very _____.

access   infrastructure   capacity   costly   function

development   decision   building   depends   availability

2   Fill in the spaces in the mind map of infrastructure. Some of the spaces are for types of infrastructure and some are for what you would use the infrastructure for.

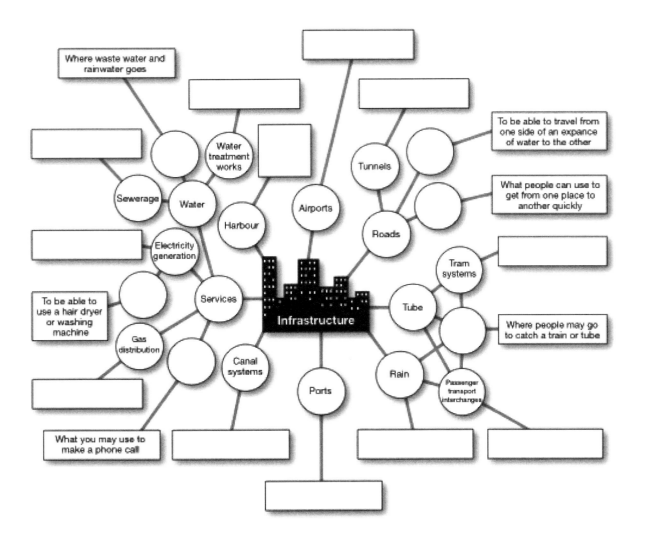

1.3   Factors influencing design and development 1

Student Book pp 8–9

1   Cut out the tiles and arrange them in the correct order for the construction cycle. Stick the arrow on your page first and stick the tiles on top in order, from start to finish.

The local council checks the design to ensure that it meets building regulations.

Planning

The artitect produces drawings of the buildings.

Building control

Buildings often have a change of use at some time within their useful life and will require changes to be made to the layout.

Construction period

This is work done during the life of the building that is carried out to ensure that the building remains in good condition.

Demolition

This is when the client tells the architect what needs building.

This is the time on site when the project is built.

Maintenance

The local council gives permission for the building to be built.

Design

Client brief

Refurbishment and conservation

Recycling
The reuse pf material following demolition.

What happens to a building at the end of its useful life.

1.4   Factors influencing design and development 2

**Student Book
pp 10–11**

1   Some areas of the country have funding from the local government to enable building to take place. Grants and support schemes are available in certain areas to support certain types of building. Find out what types of grants and support schemes for building are available in your local area. If you cannot find anything for your specific area, widen your search to the county you live in.

Present the information you find in an interesting way. Choose a method from the list below, or devise your own:

- PowerPoint presentation
- poster
- leaflet
- flyer
- report
- advertisement

2   Investigate in your local area. Where can you find any of the following?

- protected 'non-building land'
- brownfield sites
- greenfield sites.

Make a list of your findings. Are there any patterns? If so, make a note of what sorts of sites appear in which areas.

3   Draw up and complete a table, comparing the advantages and disadvantages of using brownfield sites or greenfield sites for development.

1.5   The impact of infrastructure and utility provision on development

Student Book
pp 12–13

1   You work for a housing association as an assistant in the planning department. Your company has just bought some agricultural land outside of the town that you live in. This land has just had its status changed within the local plan. Its previous use has now been changed into land that can be developed for residential use. This has made this land a very attractive investment for your company.

You have been asked to investigate what infrastructure will be required for such a development. Name six potential issues which will need to be addressed.

_____

_____

_____

_____

_____

_____

_____

_____

2   Correctly match the factors against the right infrastructure item

Drainage	Size of the existing cable supply
Water services	Nearest junction box
Roads	Types of bin
Rubbish collection	Traffic volumes
Telephones	The mains pressure
Electricity service	The location of the treatment plant

1.6   Town and country planning

Student Book
pp 14–15

1   Which of the following planning statements are true, and which are false? Write true or false against each statement.

■   The local plan only shows where housing can be constructed within your local authority's boundaries. _____

■   There are two types of planning permission: outline and full. _____

■   Planning permission is needed for any development. _____

■   You do not have to submit drawings with a planning application. _____

■   You do not need an architect to submit an application – you can do it yourself.

_____

■   Planning permission takes two weeks to complete through to a decision. _____

2   You own a large detached house that is within a conservation area. It is an area of historic beauty, which must be protected for the benefit of all the local community.

You have applied for planning permission to split the large garden at the rear of your property into two parts. One of these parts will be sold off as a building plot for development. There are several 200-year-old trees on this piece of land, which are now earmarked for felling.

Several of the neighbours have objected to this development, especially over the removal of such old trees.

Do some research on this aspect of planning permission. What arguments might the objectors use? How would you counter their objections? What arguments would you use to ensure that your application stood the best chance of going through?

3   Identify a part of your town, village or city where you feel the town planners have not quite got it right. Perhaps the development does not blend in with the surrounding environment, or some feature creates an eyesore.

Imagine you are writing a brief item for the local newspaper. They have asked you to consider what you would do to improve this situation. What future proposal would you come up with to enhance the existing unsightly development?

The newspaper has asked you to create a thought-provoking piece, and not to be scared of saying exactly what you think. They do, however, want your suggested improvements to be genuine possibilities, which should please as much of the local community as possible – not just fantasy!

1.7   The need for building regulation

Student Book
pp 16–17

1   You have designed your own extension to your house and your plan has been granted local authority planning permission. This is a small extension to your kitchen and is in keeping with the existing house and the built environment. You have started work on the extension, and have excavated the foundations to the correct depth. The building control officer has inspected these and passed them fit for purpose.

You have completed the floor slab including the insulation to the floor and have now started the outside walls. These consist of a brick outer skin with 100 mm cavity filled with insulation and a 100 mm inner skin of high-insulation blockwork.

You have just reached the damp-proof course level when the building control officer visits the site for an inspection. The officer comments: 'I do not like the colour of the brick you are using. Please change it.'

Can this officer make you change the colour of the brick? Discuss this in small teams after doing some research, and provide a shared answer.

2   You have just started working as an assistant to the architect in a design office. It is your job to make sure that the designs produced meet the current Building Regulations. Wanting to test your abilities, the architect has given you a list of the regulations – but the letters in front of the regulations have been swapped around.

Complete the architect's test by linking the letters to the correct sections.

A	Conservation of fuel and power
B	Drainage and waste disposal
C	Hygiene
D	Electrical safety
E	Resistance to the passage of sound
F	Ventilation
G	Site preparation and resistance to contaminants and moisture
H	Fire safety
J	Combustion appliances and fuel storage systems
K	Protection from falling, collision and impact
L	Structure
M	Access to and use of buildings
N	Glazing – safety in relation to impact, opening and cleaning
P	Toxic substances

3   You have just started working as an assistant building control officer with the local authority building control office. You have been there for over a week when the senior officer asks you to attend a site visit to a local housing association, which is building ten houses.

Which of the following equipment would you bring with you?

- Laser level

- Digital camera

- A set of the regulations

- The housing association drawings and specification

- A set of ladders

- A thermometer

1.8   Community consultations

Student Book
pp 18–19

1   Read the following case study then do the tasks that follow.

A major new mixed residential, commercial and retail project is proposed for the area of land between the A1M motorway and the existing community of Scawsby on the outskirts of Doncaster. Find this area on a map. The area extends to approximately 2 km^2 and covers areas of existing farmland and natural woodland. It is proposed that 3000 new homes, a small business park and a shopping arcade will be incorporated into the development. The site includes the natural habitat of many species of wildlife including birds, mammals, reptiles and fish. The existing drainage infrastructure may struggle to cope with additional surface water runoff as there is a history of localised flooding after exceptionally inclement weather.

■   Mind map your initial thoughts of what concerns there may be about this development, from the local community and from environmentalists.

■   Design a survey or questionnaire to find out what the concerns of the local community might be.

1.9　Technical information used by the designer

Student Book
pp 20–21

1　In pairs, using a range of resources, investigate and write down as many British Standards as you can, relating to materials that are used in construction. Put them in alphabetical order to help your understanding of them.

_____

_____

_____

2　In groups of four, test the following materials to find out different technical information. All the following materials should be pre-cut to the same size.

- Pine 5 mm thickness

- MDF 6 mm sheet

- Oak 5 mm thickness

Types of tests that could be carried out and measured are as follows:

- Weigh the materials to find out which is most dense.

- Bridge the materials over a gap of 300 mm, and put weights onto the materials until they snap. Record the weight that broke the materials.

- Cut the materials to find out which is the hardest to cut.

3　Look at this picture of a house. Label where technical information has been needed to build it successfully. This may be linked to the materials used, to the location of the building, or to the tolerances that have had to be taken into consideration.

1.10   Technical information sources

Student Book
pp 22–23

1   You have been approached by a private client to undertake the design of a prestigious inner-city office complex development, on the side of the river walkway. This is an attractive development with many potential clients wanting to rent office space in the multi-storey complex.

The chief designer has asked for your help in producing the high quality specifications for the materials to be used for the office interiors.

■   What factors will you take into account when deciding what to specify?

■   Where will you obtain the material specifications?

■   Is there a national standard you can specify?

2   From the following list, select the material properties that you would want to specify for a facing brick.

■   softness   ■   short lifespan

■   colour   ■   frost resistant

■   strength   ■   availability

■   range of sizes   ■   flexibility

■   weight

3   Place the missing words in the correct place in this paragraph about specification.

The specification of construction materials is an important function in any _____.

The _____ of materials in the completed design has to withstand many of the

climate's elements. These are the _____, sunshine, rainwater, _____ and

freezing temperatures. These will all contribute to the _____ expectancy of the

material.

wind   life   frost   use   design

1.11   Utility services distribution

**Student Book
pp XX-XX**

1   By drawing lines between the boxes, match the correct colour to each utility.

Electric	Yellow
Water	Green
Telephone	Blue
Gas	Black

2   The installation of the UK's infrastructure has a great impact on the local environment. For each of the following items, identify an impact that it will have:

■ Installation of electricity pylons.

■ Installation of 300 mm diameter gas main.

■ Development of a water reservoir.

■ Installation of a wind turbine farm off shore.

2

Design the Built Environment: Materials and Structures

This unit investigates the materials that used in the construction of buildings and structures. The properties and final function of the materials are examined with a focus on their performance whilst in place. The combining of different materials to make a further element is also investigated, e.g. the use of steelwork and concrete in constructing frameworks.

The use of these materials in a building is carefully considered, as is the manufacturing process of materials through to their delivery to the construction site in their final form. Many materials have to be prepared and mixed before their final inclusion within the finished building.

The second part of this unit investigates and examines the sustainable use of building materials included in a final project. More than ever we need to carefully consider the environment and the harm that we may cause by specifying a high energy polluting material into a project. Sustainable development is now a common theme in modern construction techniques. The use of recycled materials such as crushed demolition hardcore fill and engineered timber products now provide a sustainable alternative to extracting and using raw finite materials. Timber products from managed sources of timber should be encouraged and the rise in the use of cedar external cladding is a testament to this sustainable approach.

The student must also consider the amount of energy used to manufacture and use a material and how to get material to a site. The use of local materials can save on transport and distribution. Architects and designers need to make maximum use of the standard sizes of a material when dimensioning layouts, to keep waste at a small percentage as any material left in a skip is waste and has cost the environment.

The last and final part of this unit examines the building structure that holds up the walls, floors and roof. Various forms of modern construction are examined by the student. These include the structural frame of beams and columns, portal frames, shell structures, cross wall construction and finally cellular buildings. This enables the student to examine the benefits of the different forms of construction and their selection for a project. This learning is best suited to a scenario building, where the frame has to be selected, detailed and has to perform under its design considerations.

Links with other units

This unit links closely with the following units:

Level 1
- Unit 4: Create the Built Environment: Methods and Materials
- Unit 7: Modern Methods of Construction

Topics covered	Edexcel unit learning outcomes
Materials and their components	Know about materials and their function within structures
Sustainable design practice	Understand how to use materials in a sustainable way
Types of structure	Be able to evaluate and use different structural forms

How this unit will be assessed

Assessment is based on the student being able to demonstrate that they have met three areas of learning outcomes. These are:

LO.2.1 Know about materials and their function within structures

LO.2.2 Understand how to use materials in a sustainable way

LO.2.3 Be able to evaluate and use different structural forms

Marks are awarded across three banded levels with an increasing amount of evidence required to meet the higher band three outcomes. These are clearly specified in the assessment marking table within the specification.

Marks are awarded based upon the depth of knowledge a student demonstrates in each of the focus areas. This means they could theoretically achieve top marks in one assessment focus and a score of nil in another. Assessment foci are marked in three bands: band 1 generally asks the student to 'briefly describe' or 'evaluate', band 2 asks for 'descriptions', band 3 asks for 'explanation and justification'. Assessment should be based on a 'best fit' approach to the grid.

Suggested assessment

The learning outcomes for this unit will be assessed within one task which has three parts. In this assessment the student is to act in the role of the junior partner of a design practice with experience and knowledge in the specialism of sustainable design practice.

The evidence must be clearly laid out and presented using word processing packages.

The scenario puts the student in the position of having been appointed by a client to design the commission of a new building for them. The student has been asked to undertake some investigative research on the design, detailing and specification of new buildings. This is so that the client can ensure that all the materials specified by the design team are from sustainable sources and have minimum impact on the environment.

The student will be supplied with all the relevant information for this proposed local project namely:

- a description of the proposed project details
- drawings and details of the project
- a specification.

The student must produce a written technical report about the project which must include the following:

1. How materials are incorporated into the project and their function within the overall design solution.
2. An analysis of sustainability issues including the benefits and drawbacks of the materials specified and/or used on the project.
3. An investigation of the structural form adopted by the design, alternative types of structure that could be considered and analysis of the design detailing.

The student must produce a written report in A4 word processed format. Any drawings should be smaller than A3 size. Each page of the report should be numbered and include the student's name.

Learning Outcome 2.1: Know about materials and their function within structures

Students need to investigate how materials are incorporated into the project and their function within the overall design solution.

What guidance will you give?

Students need to be made aware of the sustainable element of this learning outcome in their choice of materials they investigate. The use and function of a wide variety of materials for external envelope use should be explored. Finally the overall design concept must be carefully considered in the final material selection.

What should you look for in marking?

The marking matrix is quite specific in what should be provided for this learning outcome across the three banded squares and reference should be made to this for the student's evidence. The research should include the materials performance functions in both the envelope and the structure to include insulation and fire protection as well as aesthetics.

What gains higher assessment marks?

The student needs to provide a clear description of all the key materials forming the major structural elements and external envelope. The use of the material must be justified. An evaluation of the materials function must be included. Finally a wide range of construction elements is examined in detail in combining materials with performance in use.

How could students present the evidence?

Information should be presented in the form of a written report. Drawings and sketches should be no larger than A3.

Learning Outcome 2.2: Understand how to use materials in a sustainable way

An analysis of sustainability issues including the benefits and drawbacks of the materials specified and/or used on the project.

What guidance will you give?

The student should closely examine sustainability and the issues it presents in making the best selection of materials for a given project. The environmental issues of protection and sustainability of resources must be considered. The use of recycled and reclaimed materials, timber and its products, wastage, and energy reduction materials needs to be covered. The manufacturing and processing of these materials is also an important part of sustainability. Finally the incorporation of these sustainable materials into the final project must be closely considered.

What should you look for in marking?

You need to identify sustainable materials within the project. A description needs to include the benefits or advantages and disadvantages of key materials, in terms of sustainability, that have been specified for the project.

What gains higher assessment marks?

The student needs to provide a clear description of a range of sustainable materials and justify the selection of each particular material. A detailed analysis of the benefits and drawbacks of the key materials must be included along with the effect on the environment of their use.

How could students present the evidence?

Information should be presented in the form of a written report. Drawings and sketches should be no larger than A3.

Learning Outcome 2.2: Be able to evaluate and use different structural forms

The student will conduct an investigation of the structural form adopted by the design, any alternative types of structure that could be considered and an analysis of the design detailing.

What guidance will you give?

This outcome investigates the various types of structures including framed, shell, crosswall and cellular methods of constructing the load bearing frame. The student needs to consider the advantages and disadvantages of each type of framework and the materials that are used to commonly construct them. The common forms of traditional structures are investigated along with the many components in common use.

What should you look for in marking?

The student should be able to identify the structural form used for the project and be able to describe a suitable alternative that could be used instead. This is to include construction details of the framework.

What gains higher assessment marks?

The student needs to describe as well as identify the structural form for the project. An alternative range of structural forms that could have been used needs to be described in detail, with advantages and disadvantages of each. The student will need to select, analyse and describe clearly a range of construction details.

How could students present the evidence?

Information should be presented in the form of a written report. Drawings and sketches should be no larger than A3.

Delivering this unit

This unit is best delivered with the use of an examination of the local materials used to construct the built environment. This will focus the student on the manufacture, use and properties of the material used within their built environment. The use of a local project will also cover the sustainability examination and the structural framework learning outcome.

The information in the student book for this unit is written in topics, each topic covering a particular learning outcome that relates to the awarding bodies specification. There are tasks at the end of each topic, some of which can be used to help with the production of the reports that have to be completed for this unit.

The activities in the ADR will reinforce students knowledge and can also be used to help build up evidence for the report.

Several of the activities are to reinforce knowledge learned in the student book and can be used to check understanding and be used as revision tools throughout this unit.

Integrating Functional Skills

Functional Skills can be applied throughout the topic both in the student book and the activities.

English – students will demonstrate their use of English throughout all the activities.

Speaking and listening – by contributing to discussions and making presentations and asking questions of outside speakers.

Reading – reading and understanding texts and using them to research and gather information.

Writing – communicating with others by using various written methods such as reports and letters.

ICT – students should be able to use ICT independently for a variety of tasks. They should be able to communicate and exchange information safely and responsibly, use the Internet for research and be able to present information in an effective and appropriate way such as producing text, images, tables, graphs and diagrams.

Personal, Learning and Thinking Skills

Some embedded uses of PLTS are incorporated in certain Edexcel assessment activities (see QCF unit summary inside the Edexcel unit specifications). However, use should be made of all opportunities to develop and enhance each students PLTS. Suitable opportunities will arise during the delivery and assessment activities for all of the elements of the Diploma. For example, the student may use their work experience to add to their PLTS experience and engagement. The development of the evidence portfolio on design will give the student the opportunity to use their personal and thinking skills in the solutions.

Linking to the Project

Some of the activities can be used as part of the students' project or can be the starting point towards gaining knowledge and information that will be developed should they wish to pursue this topic for their project. The relevant activities will point this out on the page.

Other useful resources

Work experience will further learning and understanding of how the sectors and services work together and these experiences will also aid work on the reports. In some circumstances this may be difficult to arrange therefore valuable insights can be obtained and primary evidence collected by inviting professionals in the sectors or services to visit and talk to the students as they can provide a stimulating input and enhance the learning of students.

Students should be encouraged to work in pairs or groups to gather information although they **must be aware** that they will need to produce an **individual report and project**.

Useful websites

- http://www.bsi-global.com/en/Standards-and-Publications/Industry-Sectors/Building-and-Construction/Construction-Materials/
- www.cementindustry.co.uk/
- www.ukforestpartnership.org.uk
- www.ibstock.com
- http://www.bsi-global.com/en/Standards-and-Publications/Industry-Sectors/Building-and-Cwww.trada.co.uk
- www.concrete.org.uk
- www.britglass.org.uk
- www.sustainablebuild.co.uk
- www.sustainable-development.gov.uk
- www.sustainworld.com
- www.materials.ac.uk/guides/environmental
- www.corusgroup.com
- www.uksteel.org.uk

Insert Centre
Logo Here

Scheme of work

Centre Name:

Title:

Level 2 Diploma in Construction and the Built Environment

Unit 2 Design the built environment: Materials and structures

Academic year: ....

Edexcel unit learning outcomes: Know about materials and their function within structures

Understand how to use materials in a sustainable way

Be able to evaluate and use different structural forms

Tutor/Lecturer(s) ....

SB = Student Book

ADR = Assessment and Delivery Resource

Guided learning hours: 60 GLH (45 + 15)

GLH	Outcome/topic (SB)	Content	Student activity	Resources	Link to Learning objective
3	**Types of structures**	• The three main types of structure in modern construction (solid, framed and surface) • The uses of these three types of structure • The materials that form the structures envelope	• Introduction to types of structures, and discussion of uses – present examples to students based on a list of landmarks you know • In pairs or groups students to Identify the types of structure for each landmark • Discuss what materials each consists of • Tutor-led discussion on different types of structures	• Starter activity SB p36 • Activities 1, 2 SB p37 • ADR activities p46	LO.2.1/1

	Topic	Learning content	Teaching and learning activities	Resources	LO
3	**Types of structures**	• The difference between a solid structure and a framed structure • The key materials utilised in the construction of these two structures	• Tutor-led discussion on different types of structures identified in first session • Students to research solid and framed structure examples • Students to analyze their own house and state the type of structure • Students to work in teams, discussing types of structure and preparing a presentation	• Personal learning and thinking skills SB p36 • Functional skills activity SB p37	LO.2.1/1
3	**Types of structures** **External Walls U4** **Steel Cladding U4**	• The functions of the external envelope materials • The combination of materials in the external envelope • Examine construction elements in detail	• Introduction to types of structures and link to LO 2.3 • Tutor lead discussion on the functions of the external envelope of a building • Students to research the different types of materials that could be used for cladding a building • Students to study detailed cladding drawings • Internet research on envelope materials	• Starter activity SB 76 • Functional skills activity SB p76 • Internet • Cladding diagrams	LO.2.1/2
3	**Types of structures** **External Walls U4** **Steel Cladding U4**	• Examine construction elements of different structures in detail • Explore how different materials work together to perform functions	• Examination of some examples of external construction details of a typical building • Discussion on construction details • Tutor led discussion followed by student research on good and bad detailing and problems that occur • Possible Guest speaker – Designer or Architect	• Internet • Guest speaker	LO.2.1/3
3	**Assessment Sessions**	• Students undertake the first session of assessment	• Learning Objective LO.2.1.1	• Assessment portfolio/ assignment task sheet	LO.2.1/1
3.5	**Sustainable design practice 2 – materials and components**	• How the right choice of material affects a building's sustainability • How design can help reduce waste • Why an architect should keep up to date with new developments in materials and components	• Complete starter activity: saving for the future, using this as a stimulus for discussion • Students to discuss how design can help reduce waste • Students to work in groups to draw up a specification for their school or college	• Starter activity SB p30 • ADR activity 1 p43	LO.2.2/1

3.5	**Sustainable design practice 2 – materials and components**	• Reclaimed and recycled materials • How these reduce wastage on a project • The local sourcing of materials	• Tutor led discussion on what recycle means with students researching examples of reclaimed materials • Students to undertake Internet based research on reclamation yards and how these are incorporated into a building • Discussion of methods of reducing wastage • Why source local materials? Students to research some local materials and report on the cost reasons for using these	• Activities 1 SB p31 • ADR activity 2 p43 • Internet	LO.2.2/1
3.5	**Sustainable design practice 2 – materials and components**	• The use of insulation • Air tightness of a building • Specialist glazing systems – Pilkington K Glass	• Students to research why is insulation a sustainable item and the benefits of increasing insulation levels • Discussion on the draw backs of this approach • Students to research Building regulation aspects to discover why buildings must be air tight • Introduce how can glass be sustainable • Internet research on Pilkingtons website	• Activities 2 SB p31 • Internet • Building Regulations	LO.2.2/1
2.5	**Climate change and the impact on building design**	• Introduction to the term 'climate change' and the causes of global warming • What the consequences are for building designers • How sustainable materials impact on climate change	• Tutor led discussion on climate change, causes and effects. Students to use Internet research to debate impact of climate change • Students to report on what aspects of design of current buildings will we have to change? • Students to research and discuss what sustainable materials can you use for climate change? Current examples to be identified and evaluated	• Activities 1, 2, 3 SB p39 • Personal, learning and thinking skills SB p40 • ADR activities p48 • Internet • PowerPoint slides	LO.2.2/2

2.5	**Sustainable design practice 1 – energy conservation**	• The impact the architect or building designer has on the energy efficiency of a building • How energy is saved • Alternative energy sources	• Mind-map thoughts on carbon footprint and sustainable design, then ranking issues raised in order of importance • Join tutor-led discussion on energy conservation • Students to work in small groups to investigate a building and prepare a presentation on sustainability changes that could be made to it • Students conduct independent enquiry into energy efficiency ratings	• Starter activity SB p28 • ADR activity 1 p42 • Personal learning and thinking skills SB p29	LO.2.2/2
2.5	**Sustainable design practice 1 – energy conservation**	• Eco-friendly materials • The best use of materials	• Students to research green materials and energy reducing materials after initial discussion of advantages and disadvantages • Students to produce a poster advertising the benefits of energy saving features to a modern dwelling	• Activities 1, 2, 3 SB p29 • ADR activity 2 p42 • Examples of eco materials used in construction	LO 2.2
3	**Assessment Sessions**	• Students undertake the second session of assessment	• Learning Objective LO.2.1.2	• Assessment portfolio/ assignment task sheet	LO 2.1/2
2.5	**The use of prefabrication in modern construction**	• What the term prefabrication covers • What types of prefabrication are available • The prefabricated composite material solution • What the advantages of prefabrication are	• Students to prepare initial ideas on prefabrication before whole group discussion • Extend discussion to main types and advantages of prefabrication. • Students to discuss case study • Students to research timber framed manufacturers via business websites and produce an advertising poster stressing the benefits of prefabrication	• Starter activity SB p38 • Case study activity SB p39 • Activities 1, 2, 3 SB p38 • ADR activities p47	LO. 2.1 & LO 2.2
2.5	**Sustainable urban drainage systems (SUDS)**	• The reduction of drainage materials using sustainable methods • Why SUDS techniques are necessary • The main SUDS techniques • The benefits of SUDS	• Tutor to introduce topic before students engage in tutor-led discussion based on need for SUDS • Students to select a SUDS technique and prepare a report and presentation • Students to prepare a recommendation for how SUDS could be used at their school or college and complete a poster or leaflet on any benefits	• Starter activity SB p32 • Activities 1, 2, 3 SB p32 • ADR activities p44 • PowerPoint slides	LO.2.2

Hours	Topic	Content	Learning activities	Resources	LO
3	**Financial and economic sustainability**	• The effect of ignoring climate change for our economy • The sustainability issues that must be addressed • The economic benefits of using sustainable materials • The recommendations of the Stern Report	• Students to write down their ideas on how people gain and lose from new construction before tutor led discussion • Students to research into the Stern Review and write down their findings. • Students to research into recent flooding in the UK and prepare a report on its possible future implications for the construction industry	• Starter activity SB p34 • Activities 1, 2, 3 SB p34 • ADR activities p45	LO.2.2/2
2.5	**Project Technical Report Assessment Session**	• Introduction to project outlined in Unit task • Students undertake the third session of assessment	• Discuss project outline, how materials are incorporated into the project and their function • Analyse sustainability issues including the benefits and drawbacks of materials • Investigate structural form adopted, alternatives and analysis of design detailing • Research how materials are incorporated and their function	• Proposal outline • Scenario outline • Site visit	LO 2.1,2.2,2.3
2	**Experiential learning**	• Presentation techniques • Web search criteria • Three areas of assessment	• Students to discuss writing techniques and prepare some written pieces • Students to discuss how best to present evidence • Portfolio building	• Internet access • Access to computer and PowerPoint software • List of useful websites	
3	**Structural Forms – types of alternative structures**	• The alternative sustainable structure	• Students investigate the sustainable modern methods of construction	• Internet access	LO 2.3/2
3	**Assessment Sessions**	• Students undertake the fourth session of assessment	• Learning Objective LO.2.1.2/3	• Assessment portfolio/assignment task sheet	LOl 2.1/2/3
2.5	**Structural Forms – types of alternative structures – Superstructures U4**	• An evaluation of the alternative superstructure	• Discussion and evaluation on a structural form • Advantages and disadvantages	• Examples • Internet access	LO.2.3/2
3	**Assessment Sessions**	• Students undertake the fifth session of assessment	• Learning Objective LO.2.1,2.2,2.3	• Mark scheme • Computer access • Internet access for further research	LO.2.1,2.2,2.3

Level 2 Diploma in Construction and the Built Environment

Lesson Plan 1
Unit 2: Design the built environment: Materials and structures – Types of structure

Centre name:

Tutor/lecturer(s):

Aims & objectives

- To consider the different types of structure

SB = Student Book
ADR = Assessment and Delivery Resource

Learning objectives

- All students will know what solid, frame and surface structures are LO 2.3
- Students will be able to identify the different types of structure LO 2.1/LO2.3
- Some students will be able to consider the reasons why a particular type of structure is used LO 2.3

Timings reflect one typical session within the GLH block of 3 hours allocated in the SOW

Total lesson time: 90 minutes

Timing/ Content	Teacher activity	Student activity	Resources	Individualised activity/differentiation	Personal learning and thinking skills	Functional skills
5 mins Welcome students and register	Check health and safety of the room Take a register	Enter room in accordance with normal procedures and settle quickly	Register			
10 mins Starter activity	Introduce different types of structure and explain starter activity	Listen to and take notes from teacher's explanation Complete starter activity	Starter activity SB p36	Discussion with Q&A session on types of structures. More detailed answers from more able students		
10 mins Functional skills	Explain the functional skills activity from SB p37. Ask the students to think about their own house and write a sentence describing it	Write down your thoughts on the structure of your house	Functional activity SB p37	Direction for weaker students to generate detailed answers	Spatial awareness and mental vision of planned drawing	English – write points of view clearly using appropriate language

	Teacher activity	Student activity	Resources	Differentiation	PLTS / Functional skills	English
25 mins SB Activities 1 and 2	Direct students to look at the holding down diagram Assist students with Activity 1 where appropriate	Complete Activities 1 and 2 – looking at he holding down diagram consider why the cardboard may be necessary	SB p37 Lined paper	More able students to generate more detailed diagram on plain A3 paper Less able students to be given step-by-step guidance and instructions for producing diagrams and allowed to use squared paper	Spatial awareness and mental vision of planned drawing	English – select read and understand texts and use them to gather information
25 mins Topic information	Explain information from Types of structures topic Lead discussion on the different types of structure including solid, frame and surface structures	Students to listen to teacher explanation and take notes	SB p36-37	More able students to generate more detailed notes Less able students to be given guidance on important factors and key words		
10 mins Students' thoughts Homework	Ask students their views and opinions on the topic Suggest homework	Discuss information covered in last activity Note down homework activity	Types of structure homework	Embedding knowledge for all students	ICT – access and search for ICT based information	
5 mins Plenary	Review of learning objectives	Q&A session to reflect on learning	What different types of structure are there? Where would you find them? How are they used?		Reflective students – consider what they have learnt to secure learning	

Level 2 Diploma in Construction and the Built Environment

Lesson plan 2
Unit 2: Design the built environment: Materials and structures – Prefabrication

Centre name: **Tutor/lecturer(s):**

Aims & objectives

- To consider what prefabrication is, and why it is used
- To understand how materials can be combined in a composite solution
- To understand cellular prefabricated construction

SB = Student Book
ADR = Assessment and Delivery Resource

Learning objectives   **Total lesson time:** 90 minutes

- Understand what the term prefabrication means, and what it covers LO 2.3/LO 2.1
- Understand what types of prefabrication are available LO 2.1
- The advantages of prefabrication LO 2.3

Timings reflect one typical session within the GLH block of 3 hours allocated in the SOW

Timing/ Content	Teacher activity	Student activity	Resources	Individualised activity/differentiation	Personal learning and thinking skills	Functional skills
5 mins Welcome students and register	Check health and safety of the room Take a register	Enter room in accordance with normal procedures and settle quickly	Register			
10 mins Starter activity	Introduce prefabrication Starter activity: Prefabrication saves time	Take notes on teacher's explanation Complete Starter activity: Prefabrication saves time	Starter activity SB p38	Discussion with Q&A session on prefabrication More detailed answers from more able students Less able students to be given personal guidance		

10 mins Topic information	Explain main types of prefabrication and advantages of prefabrication	Students to listen to teacher's explanation and take notes where necessary	Main types of prefabrication Advantages of prefabrication SB p38–39	More detailed notes and understanding for more able students Less able students to be given personal guidance for note taking	Recognition of different types of prefabrication (mental image)	Creation of relevant notes taken from teacher discussion
30 mins SB Case study	Explain case study: Prefabrication off site SB p39	Students to read through and work on case study	Case study SB p39 Lined paper	More able students to generate more detailed diagram on plain A3 paper Guide less able students with step-by-step instructions for producing diagrams. Let them use squared paper	Relating construction case study to vision in mind	Generation of thoughts and ideas concerning case study
20 mins SB Activities 1 and 2	Housing developer to use prefabrication in its designs Identifying a timber-framed manufacturer within your region	Activity 1 and 2 Students to write down thoughts on each activity – SB p38	Activities 1 and 2 SB p38	More able students to generate more detailed notes. Less able students to be given guidance on important factors and key words		Producing thoughts and written answers to activities
10 mins Reflective thoughts Homework	Ask students' views and opinions on case study Suggest homework	Discuss information covered in case study Note down homework activity	Prefabrication homework	Embedding knowledge for all students		
5 mins Plenary	Review of learning objectives	Q&A session to reflect on learning	Different types of prefabrication and the advantages of using them	Embedding knowledge for all students	Reflective students – consider what they have learnt to secure learning	

2.1   Sustainable design practice 1

Student Book
pp 28–29

1   In small groups, investigate a building that you are familiar with.

Think about:

■ how it could be more energy efficient

■ how the building is heated

■ where it loses most of its heat from

■ the different ways in which the building could be improved.

Prepare a presentation to show your findings. The presentation could be in the form of a PowerPoint, leaflet, poster or presentation board.

2   Visit www.google.co.uk/ig or search the internet to work out your home's carbon footprint. In small groups, compare your individual carbon footprints. Create a graph to show who is the most energy efficient.

2.2   Sustainable design practice 2

Student Book
pp 30–31

1   Imagine that the school or college you go to is being rebuilt, and work is in the early planning stages. You have been asked to draw up a specification for the building in terms of materials and components. List the specification points and give reasons for your decisions.

2   The left-hand column of this table lists the key features of sustainable buildings. Complete the right-hand column by describing ways in which these key features might be achieved.

Key feature	How this is achieved in a building
Designed for minimum waste	
Have lean construction and minimum waste in construction	
Minimise energy in construction and use	
Do not pollute	
Preserve and enhance biodiversity	
Conserve water resources	
Respect the local environment	

2.3   Sustainable urban drainage systems (SUDS)

Student Book
pp 32–33

1   Match up the following terms with their correct meaning.

Terms	Meanings
Filter strips	A basin that has a permanent pool of water
Swales	The roof of a building covered by vegetation, providing protection, waterproofing and insulation
Infiltration	Designed to convey and store the surface water runoff, these are broad shallow channels covered by grass
Impervious	Percolation of water into the ground
Runoff	Allows water to pass through
Porous	Wide, sloping areas of grass or other vegetation that treat the runoff from adjacent impermeable areas
Green roof	Does not allow the water to pass through
Wet pond	The water flowing off an impermeable surface

2   In pairs, consider what the benefits of SUDS are.

  ■ Make a list.

  ■ Produce a leaflet outlining these benefits.

2.4   Financial and economic sustainability

**Student Book
pp 34–35**

1   The contracts manager is concerned about the amount of wastage that is been produced on the current project that you are working on. This person has asked you to look into the economic and financial aspects of this waste, and to produce a bullet-point plan of what the company should do to reduce the problem.

Identify four ways in which wastage could be reduced on this building project.

2007 SET TO BE 'PROBABLY WETTEST UK SUMMER'

Torrential rain across the UK is likely to mean that the summer of 2007 will have been the wettest since records began in 1914, Met Office figures suggest.

Provisional tallies show a total of 358.5mm (14.1in) of rain fell on the UK, narrowly beating the previous 1956 record of 358.4mm.

2   Flooding in 2007 was a big issue for some homeowners. They were faced with several financial costs due to the excessive rainfall that occurred in the summer. This meant that the local authorities faced financial costs in connection with preventing this from reoccurring in future years. Identify four such costs associated with this work.

3   We can design our houses to reduce our reliance on the fossil fuels normally used to heat them. What can we do to house designs to help lessen their contribution to global warming?

    a   This text has some ideas, but some of the words are missing. Fill in the missing words.

        We can increase the level of i_ _ _ _ _ _ _ _ _ in the homes.

        The houses can be built mainly facing _ _ _ _ _ to catch light.

        S_ _ _ _ _ _ _ _ _ materials can be used in their construction.

        _ _ _ _ _ _ -framed construction can be used in the design.

    b   What other ways can you think of, or find out about? Look for three more ways in which house design could lessen its contribution to global warming.

2.5   Types of structure

Student Book
pp 36–37

1   **Odd one out!** Circle the structure which is the odd one out, then explain why below.

   O₂ Arena   **bridge**   **tower crane**   **climbing frame**

   _____

   _____

   _____

2   Sketch a plan view of the inside of the top floor of a two-storey house. Show how the house is divided into cells using a cellular structure.

3   Fill in the missing words.

   There are _____ main types of structure: solid, _____ and surface structures. Solid structures are usually used for _____ buildings or buildings with a _____ span. Solid structures include _____ and cross wall structures. _____ structures include rectangular, triangulated and portal _____. This type of structure is used for a range of buildings from low to high _____ and also for _____ engineering structures such as _____. Surface structures are sometimes called _____ structures and are used to span _____ clear areas with a small amount of structural support.

2.6   The use of prefabrication in modern construction

**Student Book
pp 38–39**

1   Which of the following statements are true about prefabrication and which are false? For those that are false, provide a true statement.

    a   Timber-framed prefabrication uses steel studs and plywood facing panels.

    b   With timber-framed construction you can use any finish within reason to the outside skin.

    c   A whole house can be built in a factory and assembled on site by bolting together modules.

    d   Bricklayers are now no longer needed in prefabricated construction.

2   Read the following case study.

> The house designer at your housing association company is a real stick-in-the-mud. This person was trained some 30 years ago and doesn't believe in these 'modern methods of construction', claiming that they are not tried and tested.

Imagine you have been invited to put the case for prefabrication to a meeting at which the house designer will be present. Prepare what you are going to say, by listing the benefits of prefabrication and thinking through the arguments that the house designer might use against prefabrication.

3   The architect you are working for is very keen on timber-framed construction, but the client is not sure what this involves. Visit a timber-framed construction supplier's website and find out about the advantages of using this system. Visit any other websites you can find that offer any disadvantages of timber-framed construction. Write up your findings as a sales brochure to be used to promote these energy-efficient homes to potential buyers in the area.

2.7   Climate change and the impact on building design

Student Book
pp 40–41

1   **Case study**

> You live in a 1950s housing estate. The estate contains a lot of flats closely packed together in blocks, each block containing three concrete floors and a roof. The housing estate is near to a local river tributary that feeds a major river. There was once an open green field in the middle of the housing estate, but this has been paved over with concrete play surfaces. The flats are connected to mains drainage including the surface water. The flats are cold during the winter months, so much so that many tenants complain.
>
> Now the local authority has decided to demolish the old flats and rebuild on the site.

Think about these flats and their surrounding environment. What aspects of any new design would you consider would have to be changed in light of global warming?

_____

_____

_____

_____

_____

_____

2   You have been asked to appraise the above housing development. This has come about owing to a grant from the European Community to refurbish the flats and bring them up to a modern housing standard. You have been asked to look at what methods could be used to help with climate change. Suggest some methods for:

■ refurbishment

■ upgrading.

3

Design the Built Environment: Applying Design Principles

Unit overview

The design team is an essential part of any project. It is they who take the clients brief and turn it into a working design. In this unit the individual roles and responsibilities of the team are explored including the architect or designer, the architectural technologist, the structural engineer, the civil engineer, landscape architect, building services engineers and interior designers.

Teamwork is the key word here. Everyone involved in the design team interacts and works together towards the final design solution for a project. Good relationships are essential at this key stage of a project. The role of the professional in the design team and the progression and qualification routes to this goal will be examined by the student.

The role of the professional institutions of the RIBA (Royal Institute of British Architects), RICS (Royal Institute of Chartered Surveyors), ICE (Institute of Civil Engineers) and CIBSE (The Chartered Institution of Building Services Engineers) are explored in terms of the professional organisations that support the members of the design team.

The second part of this unit looks at the application of design knowledge to formulate a design solution for a given situation or design brief. This will give the student the opportunity to illustrate creativity in design, producing some graphical information for the design either manually or using CAD. Buildability is explored in terms of an evaluation on the design solution against the original brief.

Links with other units

This unit links closely with the following units:

Level 1
- Unit 1: Design the built environment: Design influences
- Unit 2: Design the built environment: Applying design principles

Level 2
- Unit 1: Design the built environment: The design process

Level 3
- Unit 1: Design the built environment: The design factors
- Unit 2: Design the built environment: Stages in the design and planning processes

49

Topics covered	Edexcel unit learning outcomes
Job roles	Understand job roles, and the importance of teamwork, and occupational structures in construction design and related activities
Design teams and building structures	Be able to create from a brief and evaluate a realistic design solution for a typical modern building or structure.

How this unit will be assessed

Assessment is based on the student being able to demonstrate that they have met two areas of learning outcomes. These are:

LO.3.1 Understand job roles, and the importance of teamwork, and occupational structures in construction design and related activities

LO.3.2 Be able to create from a brief and evaluate a realistic design solution for a typical modern building or structure

Marks are awarded across three banded levels with an increasing amount of evidence required to meet the higher band three outcomes. These are clearly specified in the assessment marking table within the specification.

Marks are awarded based upon the depth of knowledge a student demonstrates in each of the focus areas. This means they could theoretically achieve top marks in one assessment focus and a score of nil in another. Assessment foci are marked in three bands: band 1 generally asks the student to 'briefly describe' or 'evaluate', band 2 asks for 'descriptions', band 3 asks for 'explanation and justification'. Assessment should be based on a 'best fit' approach to the grid.

This assessment is divided into two tasks that are activity based which cover the two learning outcomes as follows. The student must produce a written report in A4 word processed format. Any drawings should be smaller than A3 size. Each page of the report should be numbered and include the student's name.

Learning Outcome 3.2: Be able to create from a brief and evaluate a realistic design solution for a typical modern building or structure

The student will be supplied with a brief from a client for a modern construction project. The student will have to develop this brief into a detailed design. This task requires evidence of an analysis of the clients brief, some initial sketch proposals, floor plans, elevations and a cross section or exploded detail, either manually or using Computer aided design (CAD). The student will have to evaluate their final design in terms of how well it meets the clients brief. The student can if they wish produce a model of their final design.

What guidance will you give?

The client's brief needs to contain the right amount of detail for this task. It must state clear objectives for the building to meet so the student can produce a valid design solution. The student will require prior knowledge of drafting techniques so they can produce coherent drawings and sketches. Should the student produce a model it should be to the correct proportion and scale. The use of three dimensional projections would enhance the design solutions giving a realistic eye line perspective, as would the introduction of colour.

What should you look for in marking?

The student will need to illustrate and describe the final design solution, including features that will meet some of the clients needs from a supplied brief. A portfolio of design work illustrating the progress towards the final solution would present evidence to meet the marking grid. A final conclusion or self evaluation on how well it meets the design brief would complete the task.

What gains higher assessment marks?

The student will need to justify clearly the features of the final design solution. This must be of a high quality with great attention to detail. The final design must be evaluated in full against the original clients brief.

How could students present the evidence?

Information should be presented in the form of a written report. Drawings and sketches should be no larger than A3.

Learning Outcome 3.1: Understand job roles and the importance of occupational structures in construction design and related activities

This task puts the student into the role of a recruitment consultant for the construction industry who specialises in design staff. The student has been commissioned by the Government to produce some exciting and stimulating promotional material to recruit young design professionals into the industry.

This promotional material can be in any format the student considers appropriate, from a web page to a sound recording. This material must identify the various professional design roles and the organisations that support them through professional membership.

What guidance will you give?

The professional institutions of Architects, Building Services Engineers, Architectural Technicians and Structural Engineers would provide some guidance on this task. Research into construction industry recruitment would also provide key words to include in the presentation or promotional material. The material needs to be developed after some research so key facts can be used correctly to attract entrants into the industry and here direction needs to be given to the student.

What should you look for in marking?

The student should describe the key job roles within the design team, including those aspects they must consider teamwork. The professional pathway for the design team member must be included along with identification of the professional institutions.

What gains higher assessment marks?

The student needs to clearly describe and discuss all of the key job roles, the teamwork interaction and the professional progression paths. Interactions between supervisors, technical and professional will need to be explored. The professional institutions must be justified and explained.

How could students present the evidence?

Evidence must be included within the design portfolio. It should be in the form of A4 word processed documents. Should the student need to provide any drawings or sketches then they should be no larger than A3 and should also be included in the student's portfolio. The student should include in their portfolio a copy of any presentation materials, together with copies of any relevant observation records or witness statements.

Delivering this unit

This unit is best delivered around either around a real design project brief or a scenario brief that will have to be constructed for the students. This needs to be realistic for Level 2. Access to drawing equipment will be required to produce sketch plans and ideas to develop the brief further into scheme proposals.

The second outcome would benefit from the introduction of a guest speaker, particularly a designer who could discuss, by interview from the students, the role, career paths and qualifications for one of the professional routes.

The assessment requires that they provide a set of evidence, based around the three learning outcomes, that the student has researched based on the real or scenario project. Access to a live project would focus the students onto a practical solution to design issues that affect the local environment.

The information in the student book for this unit is written in topics, each topic covering a particular learning outcome that relates to the awarding bodies specification. There are tasks at the end of each topic, some of which can be used to help with the production of the reports that have to be completed for this unit.

The activities in the ADR will reinforce students knowledge and can also be used to help build up evidence for the report.

Several of the activities are to reinforce knowledge learned in the student book and can be used to check understanding and be used as revision tools throughout this unit.

Integrating Functional Skills

Functional Skills can be applied throughout the topic both in the student book and the activities.

English – students will demonstrate their use of English throughout all the activities.

Speaking and listening – by contributing to discussions and making presentations and asking questions of outside speakers.

Reading – reading and understanding texts and using them to research and gather information.

Writing – communicating with others by using various written methods such as reports and letters.

ICT – students should be able to use ICT independently for a variety of tasks. They should be able to communicate and exchange information safely and responsibly., use the Internet for research and be able to present information in an effective and appropriate way such as producing text, images, tables, graphs and diagrams.

Personal, Learning and Thinking Skills

Some embedded uses of PLTS are incorporated in certain Edexcel assessment activities (see QCF unit summary inside the Edexcel unit specifications). However, use should be made of all opportunities to develop and enhance each students PLTS. Suitable opportunities will arise during the delivery and assessment activities for all of the elements of the Diploma. For example, the student may use their work experience to add to their PLTS experience and engagement. The development of the evidence portfolio on design will give the student the opportunity to use their personal and thinking skills in the solutions.

Linking to the Project

Some of the activities can be used as part of the students' project or can be the starting point towards gaining knowledge and information that will be developed should they wish to pursue this topic for their project. The relevant activities will point this out on the page.

Other useful resources

Work experience will further learning and understanding of how the sectors and services work together and these experiences will also aid work on the reports. In some circumstances this may be difficult to arrange therefore valuable insights can be obtained and primary evidence collected by inviting professionals in the sectors or services to visit and talk to the students as they can provide a stimulating input and enhance the learning of students.

Students should be encouraged to work in pairs or groups to gather information although they **must be aware** that they will need to produce an **individual report and project**.

Useful websites

- www.architecture.com
- www.ciat.org.uk
- www.rics.org
- www.cibse.org
- www.ice.org.uk
- www.ciob.org.uk
- www.constructingexcellence.org.uk/resources/themes/internal/teamworking

Insert Centre
Logo Here

Scheme of work

Title:

Centre Name:

Level 2 Diploma Construction and the Built Environment
Unit 3 Design the built environment: Applying design principles

Edexcel unit learning outcome: Understand job roles, and the importance of teamwork, and occupational structures in construction design and
related activities

Be able to create from a brief and evaluate a realistic design solution for a typical modern building or structure

Academic year: ....

Guided learning hours: 60 GLH (45 + 15)

Tutor/Lecturer(s) ....
SB = Student Book
ADR = Assessment and Delivery Resource

GLH	Outcome/topic	Content	Student activity	Resources	Link to Learning objective
2	**Job roles and responsibilities – the design team**	• What is the design team • What job roles are involved within the design team? • Other professionals concerned with the design process	• Students list all those they can think of who may be involved in the design team leading into a tutor led discussion on different job roles • Research different job roles and brainstorm each one mentioned within topic • Students select two of the roles for further investigation	• Starter activity SB p48 • Activity 1 SB p48 • PowerPoint slides	LO 3.1/1
2	**Job roles and responsibilities – the design team**	• Relationships and teamwork within the design team • The different professionals within the design team • Professional progression routes • The professional qualification route	• Students to identify the different design professionals within the design team • Research on progression routes from trainee to professional. Identify how to become a professional • Students to imagine their own design project and describe the job roles involved at each point	• Activity 2 SB p48	LO 3.1/1

	Topic	Content	Activities	Resources	LO
2	Job roles and responsibilities – the design team	• The role of the Architect or Designer • The architectural technologists role • The structural engineer role • The Civil Engineer	• Q+A for students on the role of the architect • Discuss examples of famous architects, supplying material for discussion • Students to research what the structural engineer and civil engineer do in their job role.	• Examples of famous architects • Internet access	LO 3.1/1
3	Assessment Sessions	• Students undertake the first session of assessment	• Learning Objective LO.3.1.1	• Assessment portfolio/assignment task sheet	LO 3.1/1
2	Job roles and responsibilities – the design team	• The Highway Engineer • The Landscape Architect • The Building Services Engineer	• Students to identify of the role of the highway engineer • Discussion on Landscape architecture and its interaction with the main designer • Identify what services will required designing • Students to research the interaction of the services design within the team	• Internet access	LO 3.1/1
2	Job roles and responsibilities – the design team	• The Interior Designer • The role of the professionals through to completion of the building • The role of the client	• Tutor led debate on what an interior designer does. Students to discuss post design roles and how they change over time • The client, identification of their involvement in the design and interaction with the team • CDM web based research on clients legal duties		LO 3.1/1
2	Job roles and responsibilities – the design team	• The Quantity Survey • The Planning Consultant • The Facilities Manager and Property Professionals	• Research who employs the QS and the function a planning consultant has in the design team • Web based research on planning consultants • Students to complete missing words exercise on careers • Students to select two job roles and prepare a presentation on what they involve	• ADR Activities p64	LO 3.1/1
3	Assessment Sessions	• Students undertake the second session of assessment	• Learning Objective LO.3.1.1	• Assessment portfolio/assignment task sheet	LO 3.1/1

	Topic	Content	Activities	Resources	LO ref
2	**Job roles and responsibilities – the design team**	The Identification of the various Professional Institutions covering the design team • The RIBA • The CIOB • The RICS • The ICE • The CIBSIE	• Tutor led discussion on what a professional institution does for its members • Students to research why professionals join such an organisation • Web based location of one PI • Research on the role for its members	• Internet access	LO.3.1/2
3	**Assessment Sessions**	• Students undertake the third session of assessment	• Learning Objective LO.3.1.2	• Assessment portfolio/assignment task sheet	LO 3.1/2
3	**Classifications of buildings and structures**	• The definition of 'building' • The number of storeys involved in high, medium and low buildings • Categories used when classifying buildings and structures by purpose	• Students create initial mind map of types of building • Students collect a range of images of different buildings and structures and define how to categorise them • Students complete matching exercise, of function against building type	• Starter activity SB p44 • Activities 1, 2, 3 SB p45 • ADR activity 1 p62	LO 3.2/1
3	**Building design**	• Types of information needed to successfully design a building or number of buildings • The face of building design • The clients brief	• Students create a mind map based around 'design' before a tutor-led discussion • Students write a paragraph on how building design has changed over the past 50 years • Students to research a brief • Prepare and present a presentation on a particular style of housing	• Starter activity SB p46 • Activity 1 SB p47 • ADR activity 1 p63	LO 3.2/2
3	**Building design**	• How buildings are designed to either fit into the surrounding environment or make an impact upon the landscape it is placed in	• Internet research good examples of built environment design • Research and discuss Inner city regeneration – Birmingham & Glasgow • Students to research a range of buildings from across Europe and comment on appearance • Students to complete matching exercise on housing styles over several decades	• Activity SB p47 • ADR activities 2, 3 p63	LO 3.2/2
3	**Assessment Sessions**	• Students undertake the forth session of assessment	• Learning Objective LO 3.2.2	• Assessment portfolio/assignment task sheet	LO 3.2/2

	Topic	Content	Activities	LO
3	**Construction drawings**	• Construction drawings play a major part in both design and construction • Introduction to symbols and scales used • How they need to be incredibly accurate as mistakes could have dramatic consequences • Introduction to traditional drawing techniques	• Join teacher-led discussion on traditional drawing techniques including advantages and disadvantages • Introduction to design symbols, with Students using them on a drawing board • Students complete initial scale drawing • Students complete ADR activity identifying different symbols and scales	• Starter activity SB p54 • Functional skills SB p55 • ADR activities p67 • Drawing boards and material for sketch practice	LO 3.2/2
3	**Construction drawings**	• Identification of the various drawings required for planning permission and building regulation approval • Different types of drawing are used to show relevant information that is needed	• Examples of construction drawings analysed • 3D drawings and why they are used • Sketch practice working in groups on more complex drawings	• Activities 1, 2, 3 SB p55 • Examples of 3D drawings • Drawing boards and material for sketch practice	LO 3.2/2
3	**Traditional drawing techniques**	• Traditional drawing techniques still regularly used in the construction industry • Different types of drawings that can be generated, e.g. orthographic and isometric projection	• Tutor led discussion to explain why traditional drawing techniques are still used in the industry • Students to research the main types of projection used in building • Students to practice drawing a formal orthographic projection drawing, working in pencil and using correct equipment	• Starter activity SB p50 • Activity 1, 2, 3 SB p51	LO 3.2/2
3	**Traditional drawing techniques**	• Equipment that is maintained and used properly to create an accurate and effective design • Introduction to CAD drawing techniques	• Students to complete practice drawing and layout • Tutor led introduction to CAD drawing techniques with Google sketch up tutorial • Students to prepare a short flyer on CAD and prepare a sketch to support it	• ADR activities p65	LO 3.2/2
3	**Computer aided design**	• Advantages of using computer aided design • Accurate designs that are generated, with alterations that are made • How designs are made to look realistic • Drawbacks of CAD	• Tutor-led discussion on CAD drawing. Group discussion on why CAD is better than traditional techniques • Tutor to present CAD tutorial • Group exercise on basic commands within the program • Students to produce an exercise drawing, explaining differences between this process and traditional techniques	• Starter activity SB p52 • Activities 1, 2, 3 SB p52 • ADR activities p66 • PowerPoint slides • CAD program access	LO 3.2/2

2.5	**Computer aided design**	• Using CAD in place of traditional drawing techniques	• Tutor led introduction to further advanced CAD techniques • Students to complete plotting a finished drawing • Web based investigation on 3D models and how these show perspective to a client	• Internet access • CAD program access	LO 3.2/2
3	**Assessment Sessions**	• Students undertake the fifth session of assessment	• Learning Objective LO.3.1.2	• Assessment portfolio/assignment task sheet	LO 3.2
1	**Task 1 – The Design Brief**	• Client design brief given by tutor for Task 1 • Brief developed by Q+A	• Develop portfolio work • Participate in brief discussion • Q+A session so students are fully aware what is required for Task 1	• Mark scheme • Computer access • Internet access for further research	LO 3.2/2
1	**Sketch Proposals**	• Introduction to project task 1 • Sketching practice	• Students develop their skills in drawing communication of design ideas	• Proposal outline	LO 3.2/2
1	**Final Proposals**	• Presentation techniques • Web search criteria • Areas of assessment for task 2	• Students develop final proposal against the original brief • Develop final design drawings • Research and experiment with use of colour in sketches	• Internet access • Access to computer and power point • List of useful websites	LO 3.2/2
1	**Design Evaluation against brief**	• Final evaluation of sketch proposal against brief • Tutor/student 1 to 1 discussions	• Finally evaluation of design brief • Discussion on what worked and what didn't • Prepare report on this	• ICT, computer and projector • Note-taking grid • Self and peer assessment grids	LO 3.2/3
0.5	**Final Presentation Portfolio**	• Round up and summative feedback on design task	• Develop portfolio work	• Mark scheme • Computer access • Internet access for further research	LO 3.2

Level 2 Diploma in Construction and the Built Environment

Lesson plan 1

Unit 3: Design the built environment: Applying design principles – Construction drawings

Centre name: Tutor/lecturer(s):

Aims & objectives

- To understand the sorts of drawings used in the construction industry, why they are used and what they show LO.3.2

SB = Student Book 1
ADR = Assessment and Delivery Resource

Learning objectives   **Total lesson time:** 90 minutes

- Students to understand why construction drawings play a major part in both design and construction LO.3.2/1
- Students to understand why construction drawings need to be incredibly accurate as mistakes could have dramatic consequences LO.3.2/2
- Students to learn the different types of drawings that are used and what relevant information is needed LO.3.2/2

Timings reflect one typical session within the GLH block of 3 hours allocated in the SOW

Timing/ Content	Teacher activity	Student activity	Resources	Individualised activity/differentiation	Personal Learning and Thinking Skills	Functional Skills
5 mins Welcome students and register	Check health and safety of the room Take a register	Enter room in accordance with normal procedures and settle quickly	Register			
10 mins Starter	Introduction to construction drawings, why they are used, different types and why they are important	Listen to and take notes from teacher's explanation	SB p 54	Discussion with Q&A session on construction drawings		
10 mins	Neat and tidy Starter activity SB p 54	Write down your thoughts on why construction drawings need to be neat and clear	SB starter activity p 54	Direction for weaker students to generate detailed answers		

Time / Topic	Teacher content	Student activity	Resources	Differentiation	Skills	Outcomes
25 mins Functional skills Aerial drawing	Functional skills activity Aerial view of the classroom SB p 55	Create own design using scales and information taken from functional skills brief	Squared paper / plain A3	More able students to generate more detailed diagram on plain A3 paper Guide less able students with step-by-step instructions for producing diagrams. Allow them to use squared paper	Spatial awareness and vision of planned drawing	Generation of scaled drawing using accurate graphic techniques
10 mins Drawing scales	Drawing types and scales – table SB p54	Copy table into exercise book	Table from SB p 54	More able students to elaborate on the information in the table		
15 mins SB activity 3.6	Activity 1 Draw a plan view of your home Activity 2 In teams of three, produce a scaled view of the school SB p 55	Using the scale 1:50, draw a plan of the ground floor of your home In teams of three, produce a scaled drawing of the school and its grounds	SB p 55 Activities 3.6 Squared paper	More able students to generate more detailed diagram on plain A3 paper Less able students to be given guidance and step-by-step instructions for producing diagrams and allowed to use squared paper	Spatial awareness and vision of planned drawing	Generation of scaled drawing using accurate graphic techniques Work as part of a team to complete task
10 mins ADR activity 2 Homework	Teacher to explain task taken from ADR Teacher to suggest homework. Gather three different types of working drawing. Make comments about the information shown and how they differ	Complete ADR activity 2 – Fill in missing information on table shown Note down homework activity	ADR activity 2 p67	Embedding knowledge for all students		Completion of ADR activity. Students to generate correct answers to missing information
5 mins Plenary	Review of learning objectives Focus on types of drawings, what they show and why they are used	Q&A session to reflect on learning	Why are construction drawing techniques used? What is their role and importance in the construction industry?		Reflective students – consider what they have learnt to secure learning	

Level 2 Diploma in Construction and the Built Environment

Lesson plan 2

Unit 3: Design the built environment: Applying design principles – Traditional drawing techniques

Centre name: Tutor/lecturer(s):

Aims & objectives

- To consider what traditional drawing techniques are and why they are used

SB = Student Book 1
ADR = Assessment and Delivery Resource

Learning objectives

- Students to understand why traditional drawing techniques are still regularly used in the construction industry LO.3.2/1
- Students to learn why equipment needs to be maintained and used properly to create an accurate and effective design LO.3.2/2
- Students to understand the different types of drawing that can be generated using this method – orthographic and isometric projection LO3.2/2

Total lesson time: 90 minutes

Timings reflect one typical session within the GLH block of 3 hours allocated in the SOW

Timing/ Content	Teacher activity	Student activity	Resources	Individualised activity/differentiation	Personal learning and thinking skills	Functional skills
5 mins Welcome students and register	Check health and safety of the room Take a register	Enter room in accordance with normal procedures and settle quickly	Register			
10 mins Starter	Introduce traditional drawing techniques Starter activity: Why are traditional drawing techniques still used?	Discuss why traditional drawing techniques are still used today, even when CAD is available	Starter activity SB p 50	Discussion and written answer on what traditional drawing techniques are and why they are still used. Discussion allows students to understand what they are and how important they are		
10 mins Points of view	Explain the task from ADR 1 Points of view	In pairs, argue the pros and cons for traditional drawing techniques and CAD	ADR activity 1 p65	Direction for weaker students to use note-taking grids or mind mapping to organise their notes		Produce notes for use as reference when discussing pros and cons

Time / Topic	Activity	Student activity	Resources	Differentiation	Skills
25 mins Isometric drawing	ADR Activity 2: Isometric drawing	Students to generate design using isometric drawing paper	Isometric paper	More able students to generate more detailed diagram with labels. Guide less able students with step-by-step instructions for producing diagrams	Spatial awareness and mental vision of planned drawing. Generation of isometric drawing using graphic skills
10 mins Advantages/ disadvantages	Table: Advantages of using CAD or drawing boards SB p 51	Students to copy table into exercise book to cement knowledge	Table from SB p 51	Embedding knowledge for all students	Personal learning of advantages using both techniques
15 mins The drawing board	Teacher to explain ADR Activity 3: The drawing board	Role play on being a salesman, aiming to sell as many drawing boards as possible. Come up with a sales pitch to give to the class	ADR Activity 3 p65	Mind mapping ideas and generating notes for class discussion	Effective thinking skills used for generating personalised presentation. Generation of ideas and thoughts for presentation
10 mins Textbook activity and extension Activity 3.4 SB p 50	Activity 1: Why drawings are used in the construction industry. Activity 2: Main types of projection. Activity 3: Isometric projection	Activities 1, 2 and 3 Students to write down thoughts on each activity SB p 50	SB p 50 Activity 3.4 Activity 1, 2 and 3	Embedding knowledge for all students	Reflective students – consider what they have learnt to secure learning
5 mins Plenary	Review of learning objectives	Q&A session to reflect on learning	Why are traditional drawing techniques still used? What are the advantages and disadvantages?		Reflective students – consider what they have learnt to secure learning

3.1   Classification of buildings and structures

Student Book
pp 44–45

1   Match the purposes with the types of building they serve.

Residential	Where people work
Commercial	Where people go for sporting reasons
Retail	Where people go for spiritual reasons
Industrial	Where people live
Educational	Where things are manufactured
Health	Where people go to relax
Entertainment	Where goods and services are sold
Leisure	Where people go for welfare reasons
Religious	Where people go to learn

3.2   Building design

Student Book
pp 46–47

1   Pretend that you are an architect. In pairs, research a particular style of house that interests you and present it to the rest of the class, acting as the lead designer. Your aim is to try to sell the main features of the house to the rest of the class, so you have to make your chosen style of house design sound as good as possible.

Do this by presenting three design features of the property.

2   Use lines to match the correct house with the correct decade.

■ 1920s

■ 1930s

■ 1940s

■ 1950s

■ 1960s

■ 1970s

■ 1980s

■ 1990s

■ 2000s

3   Look at the photos in question 2. What changes have occurred in housing over the period? Write up your thoughts.

3.3   Job roles and responsibilities: The design team

Student Book
   pp 48–49

1   Fill in the missing words from the list below the text.

The _____ heads up and leads the design team, dealing with the initial concepts and ideas surrounding the building design. They are _____ to ensure standards are met. They also produce the initial _____ and _____ of the building.

The architectural _____ role is to _____ all the technical drawings, plans, sections and all other relevant detail to the buildings design.

Quantity _____ are the cost _____ of the construction industry. They will value the ongoing work and produce _____ and _____ of _____.

_____ engineers design the _____ and _____ of the build and ensure that the design concept works. The main areas are ensuring that the building is both _____ and capable of supporting the _____ of the building. The impact of the _____ on the build also has to be considered, so that the building can withstand _____ impacts successfully.

> **structure   quantities   weather   surveyors   architect   consultants**
> **specifications   bills   produce   stable   required   design   weight   concept**
> **technician's   structural   foundations**

2   Working in pairs, acting as careers advisors, pick two job roles from the following list and explain in detail to the rest of the class what they involve:

- Landscape architect

- Interior designer

- Electrical engineer

- Heating and mechanical drawing

- Kitchen designer

- Civil engineer

- Lighting engineer

3.4   Traditional drawing techniques

Student Book
pp 50–51

1   Working with your partner, research what CAD is. Produce a short A5 sales flyer to establish the benefits of using this type of computer design over traditional drawing techniques.

2   You have been asked to produce the sketches for a short sales flyer advertising a new home. Sketch, using a ruler and pencil, a suitable new house for this flyer.

3   Pretend you are a sales person. Your aim is to sell as many drawing boards as possible. Come up with a sales pitch to give to the class, to show why these products are so important and needed in the construction industry.

3.5   Computer aided design

Student Book
pp 52–53

1   Write down as many reasons as you can to suggest what makes computer aided design better than traditional drawing techniques.

   Do this as a class activity. Split into two groups throughout the class. One group is to produce an argument stating why traditional drawing techniques should be used; the other group does the same for computer aided design. If you wish, produce a poster or banner to highlight your group's opinions. As you go along, one member of each group should write the points made on the board, to see who has the most and best points.

2   Computer aided design has the ability to show the viewer around a building without it actually being constructed. Thinking about the house you live in, write down and describe a tour of your house as you would see it if it were designed using computer aided design.

3.6   Construction Drawings

Student Book
   pp 52–53

1   Enter the correct scale(s) used for each type of drawing.

No	Drawing type	Scale(s)	
1	Detail drawings		
2	Setting out drawings		
3	Section detail drawing		

2   Draw the layout of your classroom, with key features, using an appropriate scale.

3   In the table, fill in the name of the material each symbol represents.

Symbol	Material

4

Create the Built Environment: Structures

This unit explores the construction of a building from its substructure to the superstructure. Substructure covers the different types of foundations that support the loads of the building, from traditional strip foundations to modern raft foundation construction. The construction of all works below the damp proof course, including the ground floors, is explored by the student in detail. This covers the procedures involved in the construction of foundations, and ground floor slabs.

The different forms of structure that support a building and the material that can be used for these (such as steel and concrete) are investigated. Sustainability is an important topic that must be considered from the design stage to the construction and final completion of the building. The impact that a building or structure has on the environment must also be carefully considered.

Prefabrication of structures off site is a modern method of construction using wall modules, timber framed construction, trussed rafters, and complete building solutions. This sustainable method of construction reduces the impact of construction site works on the environment. It reduces waste, energy consumption, noise and transport issues and is the way forward in terms of reducing the affect of global warming on the environment.

Clear communication, both verbal and written, is a vital element in completing construction projects. The student will explore the use of drawn information and the various types of drawings. Technology is used in the modern construction project and the various forms of charts and programs are explored.

The project specification is a vital piece of documentation. It details the client's requirements for materials and final quality. This is interpreted in the contract documents by the designer or architect and finally produced in physical form by the main contractor on site.

Links with other units

This unit links closely with the following units:
Level 1
- Unit 7: Modern methods of construction

Level 2
- Unit 2: Design the built environment: Materials and structures

Topics covered	Edexcel unit learning outcomes
Foundations and structures	Know about the methods used in the construction of the main structural elements of a new building or structure
Site practice	Understand how buildings and structures can be built entirely in-situ or be part fabricated off site
Information and technology	Be able to explore different formats of graphical and written communications relating to the construction of the built environment

How this unit will be assessed

Assessment is based on the student being able to demonstrate that they have met 3 areas of learning outcomes. These are:

LO 4.1 Know about modern construction methods, materials and techniques

LO 4.2 Understand the use of sustainable materials

LO 4.3 Understand the job roles, career opportunities and progression routes, and the importance of teamwork, for those who construct the built environment

This unit is externally assessed by an examination. Students will sit an exam that contains a minimum of thirteen questions, each of which will require more than one response. Marks will be awarded up to a total of 60 for this paper.

Delivering this unit

A site visit during substructure works on site would be advantageous to the students to gain vital first hand knowledge of the construction of foundations. Material from piling contractors and other foundation specialists would further extend student's knowledge base. This learning is further extended into the erection of the building envelope – a subsequent later site visit could help this task. Samples of construction documentation will need to be obtained or developed by the tutor.

The information in the student book for this unit is written in topics, each topic covering a particular learning outcome that relates to the awarding bodies specification. There are tasks at the end of each topic, some of which can be used to help with the production of the reports that have to be completed for this unit.

The activities in the ADR will reinforce students knowledge and can also be used to help build up evidence for the report.

Several of the activities are to reinforce knowledge learned in the student book and can be used to check understanding and be used as revision tools throughout this unit.

Integrating Functional Skills

Functional Skills can be applied throughout the topic both in the student book and the activities.

English – students will demonstrate their use of English throughout all the activities.

Speaking and listening – by contributing to discussions and making presentations and asking questions of outside speakers.

Reading – reading and understanding texts and using them to research and gather information.

Writing – communicating with others by using various written methods such as reports and letters.

ICT – students should be able to use ICT independently for a variety of tasks. They should be able to communicate and exchange information safely and responsibly, use the Internet for research and be able to present information in an effective and appropriate way such as producing text, images, tables, graphs and diagrams.

Personal, Learning and Thinking Skills

Some embedded uses of PLTS are incorporated in certain Edexcel assessment activities (see QCF unit summary inside the Edexcel unit specifications). However, use should be made of all opportunities to develop and enhance each students PLTS. Suitable opportunities will arise during the delivery and assessment activities for all of the elements of the Diploma. For example, the student may use their work experience to add to their PLTS experience and engagement. The development of the evidence portfolio on design will give the student the opportunity to use their personal and thinking skills in the solutions.

Linking to the Project

Some of the activities can be used as part of the students' project or can be the starting point towards gaining knowledge and information that will be developed should they wish to pursue this topic for their project. The relevant activities will point this out on the page.

Other useful resources

Work experience will further learning and understanding of how the sectors and services work together and these experiences will also aid work on the reports. In some circumstances this may be difficult to arrange therefore valuable insights can be obtained and primary evidence collected by inviting professionals in the sectors or services to visit and talk to the students as they can provide a stimulating input and enhance the learning of students.

Students should be encouraged to work in pairs or groups to gather information although they **must be aware** that they will need to produce an **individual report and project**.

Useful websites

- www.buildstore.co.uk/materials/foundations.html
- www.offsite2007
- www.hanson.co.uk/713/offsite2007.html
- www.parliament.uk/documents/upload/postpn209.pdf
- www.channel4.com/4homes/diyandbuilding/buildinghouse/kit_homes.html
- www.timber-frame.org
- www.trada.co.uk
- www.rics.org

Scheme of work

Title: **Centre Name:**

Level 2 Diploma Construction and the built environment

Unit 4 Create the Built Environment: Structures [externally assessed unit]   **Academic year:** ....

Edexcel unit learning outcomes: Know about modern construction methods, materials and techniques

Understand the use of sustainable materials

Understand the job roles, career opportunities, progression routes, and the importance of teamwork, for those who construct the built environment

Tutor/Lecturer(s).......................   **Guided learning hours: 60 GLH (45 + 15)**

SB = Student Book

ADR = Assessment and Delivery Resource

GLH	Outcome/topic	Content	Student activity	Resources	Link to Learning objective
2	Excavations and ground-works	• Why some excavations are complex • What set stages excavation follows • What is done if the bearing capacity of the soil is poor	• Students to compile a list of issues connected to a local plot of land to use as a stimulus for tutor-led discussion • Tutor to explain stages in an excavation: take notes • Students to research 'earthwork support' and plant and prepare a written report • Differentiated missing blanks exercise	• Starter activity SB p58 • Activities 1, 2, 3 SB p59 • ADR activity p83–4	LO.4.1/1

2	**Foundations**	• The main purpose of foundations • The difference between strip and deep strip foundations • When and why earthwork support is important	• Students list different types of soil and bearing capacity as stimulus for tutor led discussion • Students work in pairs to discuss deep strip foundations then calculate a minimum width of a described foundation • Students work in pairs discuss dangers of trench excavations and produce a safety poster • Students to research in groups the use of concrete • Students complete fill in the blank exercises	• Starter activity SB p60 • Personal skills activity SB p60 • functional skills activity SB p60 • Activities 1, 2, 3 SB p61 • ADR activities p85	LO.4.1/1
2	**Raft and pile foundations**	• The two options if traditional strip foundations are unsuitable: raft and pile foundations • When each type of foundations is used • When they are used in combination	• Students to discuss and write a report on raft and pile foundations and identify advantages and disadvantages • Copy and learn pile foundation table and health and safety information • Students to consider the implications of basement construction	• Activity 1 SB p62 • Personal learning and thinking skills, SB p62 • ADR activities p86	LO.4.1/1
2	**Construction Plant**	• Why people use construction plant • What tasks is plant used for? • What effects the development of plant has had on buildings	• Tutor-led discussions on plant • Students to study in groups a local construction project and list factors affecting decisions on plant • Internet research of costs and features of plant, identifying factors that affect decisions • Site visit, followed by group work debating why plant decisions are made	• Starter activity SB p98 • Case study SB p98 • Functional skills activity SB p98 • Personal skills activity SB p99 • Activities 1, 2, 3 SB p99 • ADR activities 1, 2, 3 p108	LO.4.1/2
2	**Reinforced concrete**	• Things that go into a concrete mix • When concrete is strong, and when it is weak • How concrete is tested • Concrete finishes	• Students to work in pairs and mind-map issues connected with concrete before tutor-led discussion on concrete mixes • Students to practice using formulae to make concrete calculations • Students to identify examples of various types of concrete	• Starter activity SB p64 • functional skills 1, 2 SB p64 • Activities 1, 2 SB p65 • ADR activities p87	LO.4.1/1

	Topic	Content	Activities	Ref
2	**Substructures**	<ul><li>What a substructure is</li><li>What elements are included in a substructure</li><li>How the different types of ground floor substructure are different</li><li>Solid ground floors and suspended timber ground floors</li></ul>	<ul><li>Students to discuss in pairs elements of construction before tutor-led discussion</li><li>Discuss solid ground floors and suspended timber ground floors write down the difference and explain location of DPC</li><li>Students sketch fill patterns for materials</li><li>Students to discuss how design varies with height of building</li></ul>	<ul><li>Starter activity SB p66</li><li>Activities 1, 2 SB p67</li><li>Personal learning and thinking skills p66</li><li>ADR activities p88</li></ul> LO.4.1/4
2	**Superstructures**	<ul><li>What 'superstructure' means</li><li>Elements that make up the superstructure of a building</li><li>Why it is useful to split a building up into elements</li></ul>	<ul><li>Students to discuss what a superstructure might be before defining in a mind-map</li><li>Students study Parul case study, studying different buildings and defining the elements</li><li>Students to draw a scale drawing of room, then test their plans accuracy with a partner</li><li>Students to complete activities testing ability to identify elements</li></ul>	<ul><li>Starter activity SB p68</li><li>Case study SB p68</li><li>Activity 1 SB p69</li><li>Functional skills p68</li><li>ADR activities p89</li></ul> LO.4.1/4
2	**Steel-framed structures**	<ul><li>What a holding down bolt does</li><li>Why steelwork needs fireproofing</li><li>What a portal frame is</li><li>The construction envelope</li></ul>	<ul><li>Tutor-led discussion on possible limitations on high buildings</li><li>Students to identify features of steel-framed structures, and research their advantages and disadvantages</li><li>Students to complete short report on alternatives to steel</li><li>Students to complete activities on protecting steel framed structures</li></ul>	<ul><li>Starter activity SB p74</li><li>Activity 1 SB p74</li><li>ADR activities p92</li></ul> LO.4.1/4
2	**External walls**	<ul><li>How external walls are constructed in most houses</li><li>How external walls can protect you from the weather</li><li>Other functions external walls perform: thermal and sound insulation, security, lighting</li></ul>	<ul><li>Write down notes and discuss functions of an external wall</li><li>Students to sketch an elevation and write a short report on impact of size and positioning</li><li>Students to produce an artwork showing the functions of the external wall</li><li>Students to work in pairs and produce a presentation showing how thermal insulation takes place</li></ul>	<ul><li>Starter activity SB p70</li><li>Activities 1, 2, 3 SB p70</li><li>Functional skills p70</li><li>ADR activities p90</li><li>PowerPoint slides</li></ul> LO.4.1/5

2	**External cladding**	• How not all external walls are load-bearing and may be panels attached to a structural frame • How cladding can be prefabricated • The wide choice of external finishes • How cladding provides the protective enclosure for framed buildings	• Students to list the buildings in their area with frames and cladding • Write the advantages and disadvantages of the different types of external cladding • Investigate and write down information on different types of cladding using the internet • Complete list of advantages and disadvantages of each type of cladding • Students to work in groups to produce a powerpoint display to explain how prefab cladding is produced	• Starter activity SB p76 • Activity 1 SB p76 • Functional skills p77 • ADR activities p93	LO.4.1/5
2	**Floors**	• How floors can be either solid or suspended • How and why ground floors should be insulated • The functions floors perform • Types of floor: solid, beam and block, suspended timber	• Students to write a performance specification for a floor and mind-map functions as a group discussion • Produce a table with information and type of floor within it, including advantages and disadvantages • Students produce a 2-D sketch of a joist layout and discuss why certain joists are used • Students produce a cross sectional sketch and describe process of installation	• Starter activity SB p78 • Activity 1, 2 SB p79 • Personal learning and thinking skills p78 • ADR activities p94	LO.4.1/5
2	**Roof structures**	• How roofs can be either flat roofs or pitched roofs • How roof structures transfer loads to the supporting walls or structure • Traditional roofing terms • Roofing for framed structures	• Students write a list of possible advantages and disadvantages of supporting structures before tutor-led discussion • Students to complete a 2-D diagram of a roof • Students to investigate the differences between a rafter and trussed rafter • Label a roof diagram, naming components • Write a report on the process used to repair a roof	• Starter activity SB p80 • Activities 1, 2, 3 SB p80 • ADR activities p96–6 • PowerPoint slides	LO.4.1/5
2	**Roof coverings**	• How roof coverings provide protection from the elements • Why vapour control and ventilation are essential • Flat roofs and pitched roofs • Roof coverings for framed structures	• Students to consider the different materials roofs are made from • Take information from topic and put into own words in clear table • Students to carry out an investigation into the difference between plain and interlocking tiles • Students to investigate meaning of term 'interstitial condensation' and write a brief report • Students to produce a 'beginner's guide' to tiling	• Starter activity SB p82 • Activities 1, 2, SB p82 • Personal learning and thinking skills p83 • ADR activity p97	LO.4.1/5

	Topic	Content	Activities	
2	**Internal Partitions**	• What partitions are • How partitions are classified as load-bearing or non-load-bearing • Demountable partitions	• Students to make note of the differences between an external and internal wall • Discuss types of partitions and give their definitions, describing differences • Students to list details of demountable partition systems • Students to produce layout diagram of structural members and detailed diagram of a floor in their house • Prepare a Powerpoint presentation on the process used to construct internal partitions	• Starter activity SB p84 • Activities 1, 2 SB p85 • Functional skills p84 • ADR activities p98	LO.4.1/5
2	**Services installations**	• The five main types of service installation • How the services supplied to homes and services supplied to larger buildings vary • Why services are governed by laws and regulations	• Students to compile a mind-map showing how they use services • Prepare a brief presentation on regulations in the role of an inspector and explain why these laws are in place • Students work in groups to produce a Powerpoint presentation on a chosen regulation	• Starter activity SB p86 • Functional skills activity SB p87 • Activities 1, 2, 3 SB p87 • ADR activities p99	LO.4.1/5
2	**Plastering and dry lining**	• How plastering and dry lining are two ways to give masonry a smooth finish • Several different types of inner wall: solid, lath and plaster, dry-lined and partition	• Tutor-led discussion on plastering and dry lining. • Students to consider tools used • Students calculate number of square metres in the room • Students create a step-by-step guide explaining plaster mixing and carry out research on drying times • Students role-play plasterer scenarios	• Starter activity SB p88 • Functional skills 1 SB p88 • Activities 1, 2 SB p88 • ADR activities p100	LO.4.1/5
2	**First and second fixing**	• Why much planning is needed when considering both first and second fixings • The tools, materials and equipment needed • Why contractors have to be organised in the right way • How second fixing relies heavily on the first stage being completed properlY	• Students mind-map the difference between first and second fix before a tutor-led discussion • Students explain difference and produce a table linking job roles to fixing stage • Students to prepare a report on those professionals involved at each stage	• Starter activity SB p90 • Activities 1, 2 SB p91 • Personal learning and thinking skills SB p90 • ADR activities p101–2	LO.4.1/5

	Topic	Content	Activities	Ref
2	**Windows and doors**	• The role of windows and doors • How windows and doors can combine functionality with creating a better ambience • New materials and their impact on style and design • The ability of new materials to withstand external effects. • Sill details and weathering	• Students draw a 3-D drawing of their house and discuss placement of windows and doors. Discuss in pairs, highlighting differences between internal and external • Read and revise tables for five minutes and try to write down as much as possible without the topics • Students complete mix and match exercise	• Starter activity SB p92 • Activities 1, 2 SB p92 • ADR activities p103–4	LO.4.1/5
2	**External works, drainage and landscaping**	• What drainage is for and how it works • The differences between the sewerage system and the drainage system • Types of drainage system • What external works comprise of: boundary walls, pavements, parking areas, footpaths and gardens	• Students list features around their house and write down a definition of the three types of drainage • Students research main types of surfacing • Research and create a table showing advantages and disadvantages of the drainage systems • Write a report on any drainage or landscaping work carried out in the local area • Students complete labelling of example systems	• Starter activity SB p94 • Activities 1, 2 SB p95 • ADR activity p105–6	LO.4.1/5
2	**Demolition**	• Why demolition is a dangerous business • The main methods used in modern demolition • What factors determine the type of demolition method used • Demolition and the impact on the community	• Students consider the method of demolition for a chosen building and investigate and write down information concerning different types of demolition • Students to research why decisions are taken for demolition and prepare a short presentation • Students to consider what parts of a building could be recycled and identify sustainable demolition products	• Starter activity SB p96 • Functional skills SB p96 • Activities 1 SB p97 • ADR activities p107	LO.4.1/6
2	**Openings in external walls**	• What the function of a 'head' is • What materials lintels are made of • Why all doors and windows have sills • Jambs, arches and sills	• Students observe fronts of buildings and prepare list of observations before reading through and making notes on remaining topic information • Revise table for five minutes – write down as much information as possible that you can remember • Students investigate different types of arches and produce sketches • Students investigate different types of lintels and sills available to create a leaflet explaining the features of these • Students complete a mini report on jambs, arches and sills	• Starter activity SB p72 • Personal learning and thinking skills SB p73 • Activities 1, 2 SB p73 • ADR activities p91	LO.4.1/5

	Topic			
2	**Sustainable site practice 1 – community issues**	• The advantages of using community liaison • Site management and sustainability issues • The consequences of not adopting good site practice • Why contractors join the Considerate Contractors Scheme	• Students discuss in pairs what is involved in being a considerate constructor before a tutor-led discussion • Students research the Considerate Contractors Scheme, writing a short report and preparing a short presentation • Students produce a poster promoting sustainable site practice • Research and write a job description of a Community Liaison Officer	• Starter activity SB p106 • Personal learning and thinking skills SB p106 • Activities 1, 2 SB p107 • ADR activity p112 — LO.4.1/6
2	**Sustainable site practice 2 – environmental**	• How environmental good practices also solve community issues • How the construction industry minimises waste • What the embodied energy of a project includes	• Discuss and mind-map thoughts on uses of natural resources and the effects it may have • Copy and learn sources of embedded energy artwork from topic • Study a local construction site and list sustainable site practices used. Students to address which solve community, issues environmental issues or both • Students to write their own understanding of sustainability	• Starter activity SB p108 • Activities 1, 2, 3 SB p108 • ADR activities p113 — LO.4.1/6
2	**Prefabrication**	• Tutor directs links to SOW for Unit 2 which details prefabrication for this learning outcome	• Overlap discussion links with Unit 2 • The methods of prefabrication • Quality control • The benefits of using prefabrication on site • Site fixing techniques	• Kingspan Tek system video • Timber-framed housing guide — LO.4.2
2	**ICT applications in project management**	• What a Gantt chart is • What CAD is • What ICT methods of communication are available on a modern construction project • How ICT and programming are used together	• Students to consider retraining • Using information from topic, write down what a Gantt chat is, what CAD is and what ICT methods of communication are available on a modern construction project • Internet research into types of work program software available • Students to prepare a gantt chart for a small project • Complete matching exercise	• Starter activity SB p104 • Activities 1, 2 SB p105 • ADR activities p111 — LO.4.3/1 LO.4.3/2 LO.4.3/3

Hours	Topic	Content	Teaching activities	Resources	LO
2	**Organisation and programming**	• What a planner's main responsibilities are • How a Gantt chart is used • What a Gantt chart can tell you • Other types of programming: contract programming, computer software programs	• Students discuss main responsibilities in a tutor-led discussion and write down their thoughts • Students prepare a list of planner's roles and reasons for projects to remain on time • Students to create a gantt chart for several different projects • Students adjust gantt charts for delays	• Starter activity SB p102 • Functional skills activity SB p102 • Activities 1, 2, 3 SB p102 • For your project SB p103 • ADR activities p110	LO 4.3/3
2	**Site documentation**	• Various construction documentation identified for a typical project • Standard drawing conventions • What a bill of quantities is • Health and safety on site – legislation such as PUWER	• Students identify what a drawing register is, an architects instruction, a site diary, drawing issues, confirmation of verbal instruction, timesheets • Identification of the bill of quantities • Standard drawing convention quiz	• Samples of documentation • Sample Bill of Quantities • Drawing convention sheet	LO.4.3/4
2	**Site management**	• The site management team: project manager, site manager, site engineer, general foreman, craft operatives, general operates	• Students to consider problems that could occur on site – tutor-led discussion on who would resolve these • Students discuss case study on site management • Students work in groups to decide on the strengths and skills needed for each role • Work in pairs to draw up an organisational chart, including health and safety supervisor and lines of communication • Produce a brief job description for the recruitment of a new site personnel	• Starter activity SB p100 • Activities 1, 2 SB p100 • Case Study SB p100 • Personal learning and thinking skills SB p100 • ADR activities p109	LO 4.3/4
4	**Exam Revision Session**	• Revision of topics	• Students undertake revision study in preparation for exam		

Lesson plan 1

Unit 4: Create the built environment: Structures – Foundations

Centre name:

Tutor/lecturer(s):

Aims & objectives

- To consider what demolition is, where and when it is used, and what methods are available

SB = Student Book 1

ADR = Assessment and Delivery Resource

Learning objectives

- Students to understand the common foundation types LO.4.1/1
- Students to learn about the main methods and plant used in constructing foundations LO.4.1/2

Timings reflect one typical session within the GLH block of 3 hours allocated in the SOW

Total lesson time: 90 minutes

Timing/ Content	Teacher activity	Student activity	Resources	Individualised activity/differentiation	Personal learning and thinking skills	Functional skills
5 mins Welcome students and register	Check health and safety of the room Take a register	Enter room in accordance with normal procedures and settle quickly	Register			
5 mins Task 1 from ADR – A, B, C activity	Ask students for individual answers to flow chart Activity 4.1A	Answer tutors task for activity	ADR Activity 4.1A p83 ADR Activity 4.1B p84	More able students to work on 4.1B		Students to think of how to fill in the flow chart
10 mins Starter 'Activity 4.2'	Explain Starter activity: The foundation terms SB p60	Foundations – thinking of the function of a foundation what does it do? Different types of foundations	Paper and pens Starter activity SB p60	Discussion on what a foundation is and why it is used Less able students needing guidance with answers and thoughts Feedback process enables students to share ideas	Effective participators – able to join in discussion and communicate ideas	

Time / Topic						
20 mins The types of foundation	Strip foundations Deep Strip foundations	Listen to and take notes on tutor explanation Students to complete ADR Activity 4.3 raft and piled foundations	ADR Activity 1 p86	Direction for weaker students to use note-taking grids or mind mapping to organise their notes Students to generate a detailed list of the different foundations with sketches		Graphical detailing-drawing
25 mins Types of Construction plant in forming foundations	Give detailed explanation on different types of plant used in the construction of foundations	Watch videos on construction plant Take notes Discussion on aspects of video	Construction plant supplier video Piling video	Students to detail the different types of plant used More able students to produce more detailed explanations Less able students to be given guidance on advantages and disadvantages	Categorising information into a table format	
10 mins The range of plant and equipment available	General plant used on site for construction of the superstructure	Discussion and Q+A to draw out the different construction and materials handling plant Identify plant from pictures or video What each does or performs	Video of typical construction site	Guide roles of particular students to aid discussion Those with more confidence to organise discussion; less confident to work with others to create safe environment for voicing opinions	Using the classroom, students learn what each plant item does	
10 mins Web based research on JCB website	Identify what a 3CX is and its benefits	Students identify the JCB 3CX and its advantages	Web based search resource	Embedding knowledge for all students		Students to create and generate accurate thoughts and answers to activities
5 mins Plenary	Review of learning objectives, teacher to suggest homework activity	Q&A session to reflect on learning	Paper and pens		Reflective students – consider what they have learnt to secure learning	

Lesson plan 2

Unit 4: Create the built environment: Structures – Windows and doors

Centre name:

Tutor/lecturer(s):

Aims & objectives

- To consider the function of windows and doors.

SB = Student Book

ADR = Assessment and Delivery Resource

Learning objectives

- Students to clearly understand the purpose of windows and doors LO.4.1/5
- Students to be able to identify the different types of windows and doors and why they are used LO.4.1/5

Timings reflect one typical session within the GLH block of 3 hours allocated in the SOW

Total lesson time: 90 minutes

Timing/ Content	Teacher activity	Student activity	Resources	Individualised activity/differentiation	Personal learning and thinking skills	Functional skills
5 mins Welcome students and register	Check health and safety of the room. Take a register	Enter room in accordance with normal procedures and settle quickly	Register			
10 mins Starter	Describe purpose and function of windows and doors and where they can be located. Explain the differences between external and internal doors. Teacher to explain why different types of windows and doors are used.	Complete worksheet on different types of windows, with the aid of the tutor and the Student Book.	Paper and pens Starter Activity SB p92 – What goes where?	Feedback process enables students to share ideas		
10 mins	Explain the use of windows and doors and the different types	Students to take note from tutor explanation	SB p 92	Direction for weaker students to use note taking grids or mind mapping to organise their notes		

				More able students	Effective thinking skills	Generation of ideas
25 mins SB Activity 1 – Take a Tour.	Activity 1 – Take a Tour SB p 92	Take a tour – identification specific task	SB Activity 1 – Take a Tour p 92	More able students to produce more detailed answers for activity	Effective thinking skills used for generating personalised answers	Generation of ideas and thoughts for answers
25 mins SB Activity 2 – Types of windows and doors	Activity 2 Types of windows and doors	Windows and doors and why they are used	SB Activity 2 – Types of windows and doors p92	Give guidance on areas that need answering – explain any areas of difficulty	Students to use thinking skills and reflecting on thoughts to produce written work	
10 mins ADR activity 1 and 2	Students to complete ADR Activity 1 and 2 – The correct description	ADR activity 1 and 2 – the correct description – students complete worksheets for both activities	ADR activity 1 and 2 p103–4	Embedding knowledge for all students		Internet research can be used to help complete the activities
5 mins Plenary	Review of learning objectives	Q&A session to reflect on learning	What are the different types of windows and doors?		Reflective students – consider what they have learnt to secure learning	

4.1A   Excavations and groundworks

**Student Book
pp 58–59**

1   Fill in the missing parts of the flow chart to show how excavations are carried out.

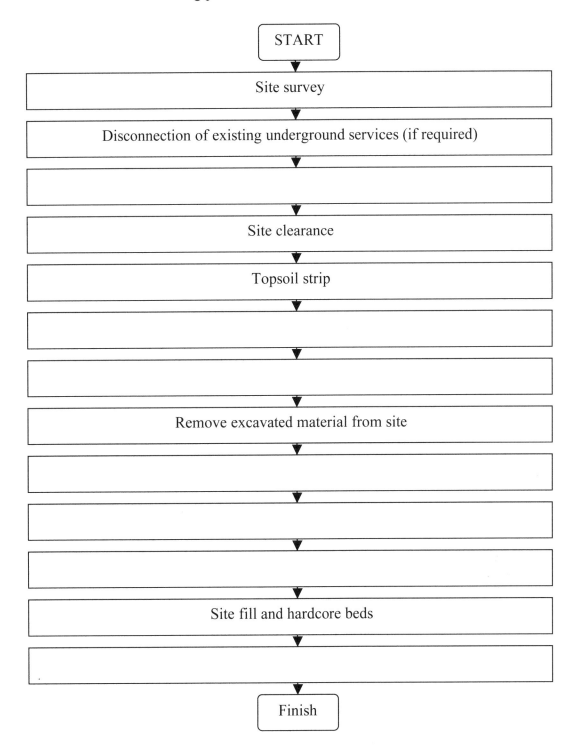

4.1B   Excavations and groundworks

Student Book
pp 58–59

1   Fill in the missing parts of the flow chart to show how excavations are carried out.

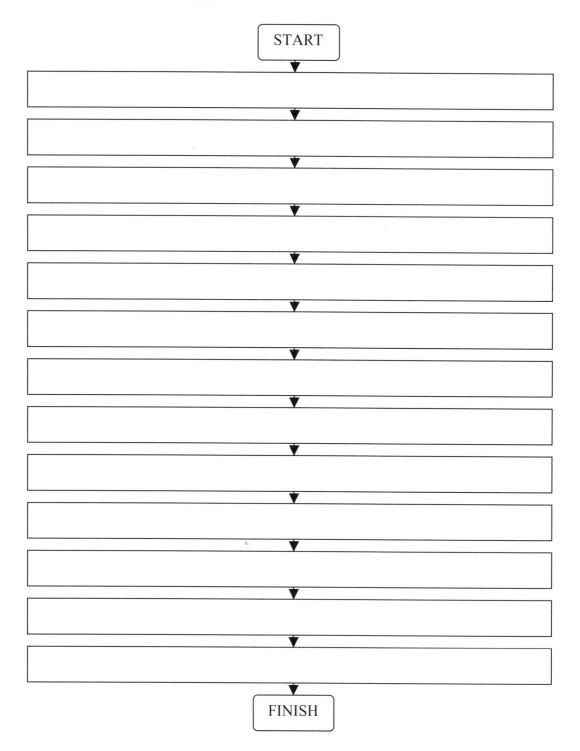

4.2   Foundations

**Student Book
pp 60–61**

1   The following paragraph has lots of words missing from it. Put these back in, from the
     list below.

> **Subsoils** can be of many different types including _____, _____, _____, silts and
> _____, and each will have a different bearing capacity and will therefore need a
> different type, size or depth of foundation. A lower bearing _____ generally
> means that foundations have to be wider, _____ or transfer loads to a suitable
> bearing stratum. Special consideration has to be given to _____ because it can be
> affected by seasonal weather changes to a depth of one metre – this means that
> _____ in clay subsoils have to be a minimum of 1m deep. Normally
> foundations have to be 750 mm deep because this is the depth that _____ can
> penetrate. Subsoils can contain water which expands when frozen; this can lead
> to 'frost heave' which is an upward _____ which could damage a
> _____ if the foundations are of insufficient _____.

rocks   sands   pressure   foundations   building   frost

clays   deeper   capacity   peats   clay   depth

2   What do the following terms mean? Put a definition after each one.

Load	
Bearing capacity	
Settlement	
Foundation	
Bearing strata	
Subsoil	
Topsoil	

4.3   Raft and pile foundations

Student Book
   pp 62–63

1   Write a report entitled 'Raft or pile?' In your report, give an explanation of:

   ■ what raft foundations are

   ■ what pile foundations are

   ■ where each type of foundation may be used.

2   Using information from the two sections on foundations add legs to the mind map to show what you know about the different types of foundations. To extend your work, do some further investigation on the Internet to add to your thoughts.

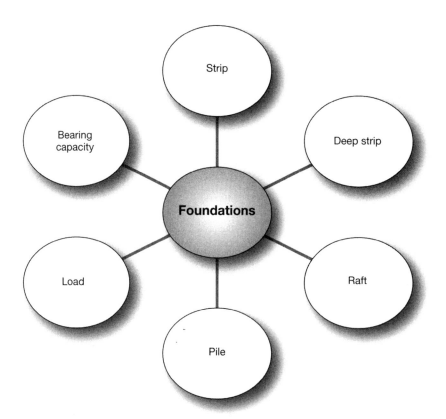

4.4   Reinforced concrete

Student Book
   pp 64–65

1   Find examples of the following types of reinforcement for concrete. Insert them into the table either by making a sketch of them or by cutting and pasting them into the table.

Type of reinforcement	Image
Square twisted bar	
Square and mesh fabric	
Ribbed bar	
Structural mesh fabric	
Twisted ribbed bar	
Plain round bar	
Long mesh fabric	

2   Design a poster or sign that could make construction workers on site aware of the safety precautions you need to take when using cement. Include what PPE is required to protect the skin from burning.

4.5   Substructures

Student Book
pp 66–67

1   Match the following words to their statements by colour coding the small box next to each word and statement.

Honeycomb		Not supporting anything other than its own weight	
Wall plate		Brickwork built ¼ bond with a ½ brick gap between each adjacent stretcher	
Non-load-bearing		A large dense area of material that retains and dissipates heat over a period of time	
Thermal mass		A softwood bearer, typically 100 mm by 50 mm, that supports the ground floor joists	

2   Identify the following materials from their fill pattern on the following construction drawing.

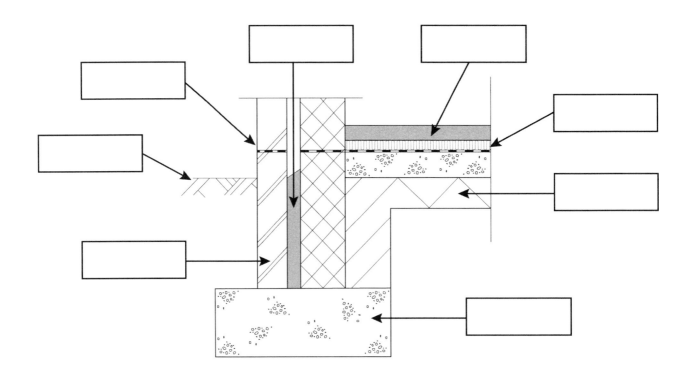

4.6   Superstructures

**Student Book
pp 68–69**

1   Here is the definition of a superstructure – but some of the words are missing. Can you find the missing words and fill them in?

A _____ is that part of a building that can normally be seen because it is _____ ground. The superstructure can be built out of many different _____ including brick, concrete, stone, _____ and glass. The main function of a superstructure is to provide a safe, _____ shelter to allow the occupants to go about their business, leisure or domestic activities in a _____ environment.

comfortable   above   steel   materials   secure   superstructure

2   Find two different images of a house: one should be an exterior view; the other should be an internal view. On the images you have chosen, label and describe the common elements that are part of the superstructure of the house. Use the following list to help you:

- External walls
- Internal partitions
- Floors
- Roof
- Windows and screens
- External doors
- Internal doors
- First fix

- Second fix
- Floor, wall and ceiling finishes
- Suspended ceilings
- Electrical installations
- Plumbing installations
- Heating and mechanical installations
- Painting and decorating

4.7   External walls

Student Book
   pp 70–71

1   Fill in the three different ways in which external walls provide weather protection and shelter from wind, rain and snow.

Method of protection 1	
Method of protection 2	
Method of protection 3	

2   In pairs, investigate how thermal insulation is carried out. Try to explain the process through the aid of diagrams, and produce a PowerPoint presentation between you. Name the tools and equipment needed.

3   Look carefully at the diagram of the section through an external cavity wall on page 71 of the student book, including labelling, for two minutes only. Now turn the image over and try to reproduce the diagram, with labels included.

4.8　Openings in external walls

Student Book
pp 72–73

1　Be an investigator for the day. Investigate different openings in external walls, either on the internet or in your local area. Under the following headings, create a mini report on each area including a photograph, image or sketch and description of what you see.

- jamb

- head

- arch

- sill

2　Using notes and sketches, describe why an arch would need temporary support while being constructed.

4.9   Steel framed structures

Student Book
pp 74–75

1   From the following list annotate the drawing of the portal frame, using the most appropriate technical terminology.

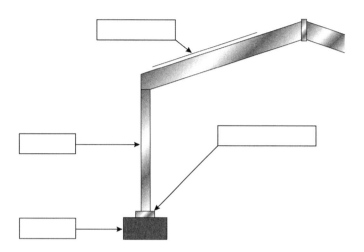

Foundation types	Foundation connection	Method of erecting	Envelope material
Pad	Screws	Winch and chains	Campsite cladding
Strip	Holding down bolts	Crane	Timber cladding
Piled	Site drilling	Air bags	Curtain walling
Raft	Cement supply	Forklift truck	Rendered blockwork

2   Identify which of the following methods protect steelwork from oxidation (rust).

- concrete cover
- using paint
- using stainless steel
- cover with plasterboard
- timber cladding

3   The risk of damage from fire in a steel-framed building has to be carefully considered, as a fire can cause steelwork to lose 50% of its strength, risking the collapse of a building.

There are many methods for protecting the steel frame from fire. Select the correct ones from this list.

- plasterboard
- concrete
- timber
- glass reinforced plastic
- glass
- gloss paint
- blockwork

4.10   External cladding

Student Book
  pp 76–77

1   Write down five 'key words' that can be associated with the following headings:

  ■ timber cladding

  ■ tile hanging

  ■ profiled steel cladding

  ■ glazed cladding

  ■ brick cladding

  ■ concrete cladding

  ■ membrane or fabric structures.

2   Create a spider diagram that shows as many different types of finishes as you can think of that can be applied to external cladding.

3   In groups of four, research and present how prefabricated cladding is produced off site. Explain the process from start to finish, using diagrams to highlight important information.

4.11   Floors

Student Book
pp 78–79

1   Produce detailed cross sectional sketch of a simple ground floor, and label it with all the functions that a floor performs.

2   Write down as much as you can about the different types of floors given in the table below. Then check in the book and write any information you have missed into the last column.

Flooring	Information I know	Information I missed
Solid floor		
Beam and block floor		
Suspended timber floor		

3   Imagine that you have been asked to construct a solid ground floor for a detached house. Describe how you would go about this process, naming tools, equipment and materials. Where would you start? What would you do? How long might it take? How would you ensure health and safety procedures were followed?

4.12   Roof structures

Student Book
pp 80–81

1   The picture below shows a structure of a roof. Using the key words, label the diagram correctly.

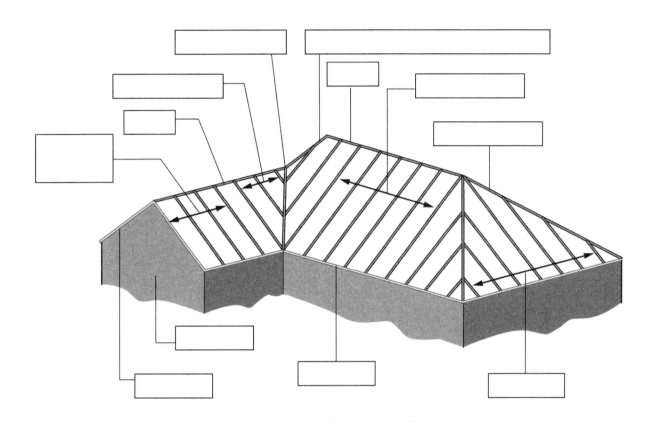

Common rafters	Verges	Eaves
Gable End	Ridge	Jack rafters
Hip rafter	Valley rafter	

2   Fill in this table.

Description	Advantages	Disadvantages
Pitched roof		
Flat roof		
Trussed rafters		

3   Produce a diagram that shows clearly how the roof transfers loads to the supporting walls or structure. Use arrows to highlight the forces involved and list what type of forces may occur.

4   Imagine that your garage roof needs replacing after a long period of wear and tear. Explain how you would go about doing this. Explain where you would start, where you would get the materials from, how you would get the cheapest prices, how you would do the task safely and what you would do with the old roof (i.e. how you would take it off and dispose of the materials). Write a passage to explain all your thoughts on how the roof can be replaced successfully.

4.13   Roof coverings

Student Book
pp 82–83

1   For each letter, find a true statement that applies to roof coverings.

R_____

O_____

O_____

F_____

C_____

O_____

V_____

E_____

R_____

I_____

N_____

G_____

2   Produce a 'beginner's guide' booklet to show how tiling should be done. You may need to do some research to ensure that the guide is both truthful and realistic. The booklet has to include references to health and safety, how materials should be stored and handled correctly, and tools and equipment that are to be used. Use diagrams to help describe certain processes and information.

4.14   Internal partitions

Student Book
pp 84–85

1   Draw a detailed plan of one floor of your house. You can draw either the ground floor or the first floor where appropriate and should show detail of the internal partitions used in your house. Label the rooms and give dimensions of internal partitions if possible.

2   Describe five differences between load-bearing and non-load-bearing partitions in the table below.

Load-bearing	Non-load-bearing

3   You have been asked to present to the future owner how you intend to construct all the internal partitions of a building. This is to be done in the form of a PowerPoint presentation. You should draw the stages of construction and when each individual partition will be put in place. Use your own house as the example, to help you visualise the partitions that will be presented.

4.15   Service installations

Student Book
pp 86–87

1   For this activity you will need to work in a group of four. Each of the people in the group researches one of these sets of regulations:

   ■ IEE Wiring Regulations 17th edition

   ■ Electricity at Work Regulations 1989

   ■ Gas Safety Regulations 1988

   ■ Water Supply Regulations (hot and cold)

   Then work together to prepare a short PowerPoint presentation to deliver to the class. Each presentation should include:

   ■ the major points of the regulations

   ■ diagrams and images to support the explanation

   ■ details of how the regulations support service installations in the UK (for example, how these regulations help to protect the customer).

2   Draw a mind map to show your understanding of the services to be installed in a two-storey residential building. Your mind map should show all the different kinds of services and what these services support (for example, electricity for heating, hairdryer, kettle, etc.)

   Draw your mind map out in rough first. Once you are happy with it, draw out a final version using different colours, underlining or sketches to aid your understanding.

4.16   Plastering and dry lining

Student Book
pp 88–89

1   Give an explanation of each term in the table below.

Solid wall	Lath and plaster wall	Dry lined wall	Partition wall

2   Work in pairs. One of you is a plasterer; the other is a client. The plasterer has been taken on to plaster the client's front room. The plasterer needs to explain clearly to the client what he/she is going to do, and in what in order, naming all the tools and materials that will be used. When you have finished, reverse roles.

3   Using a similar scenario to that in question 2, imagine that you are a plasterer who is about to plaster a room. Using your living room as the example, this time write a letter to the client, outlining what you will need to do, in what order, naming all the materials and tools that you will use.

4   Name the material you have hit if the following residue appears on the drill bit when you are drilling into a wall.

White residue; the drill bit meets some resistance then shoots forward	Any wooden dust residue	Any light grey/cream dust	Red residue	Dark grey residue

4.17 First and second fixings

Q	O	K	Z	Q	B	H	M	X	P	B	F	G	G	Q	K	N	I	H	V
D	K	S	C	E	U	T	D	K	Z	X	V	P	J	N	A	P	Q	Y	B
R	O	Q	S	U	A	A	G	K	G	I	B	X	I	Q	I	C	A	S	L
A	X	I	D	M	N	B	D	N	N	R	K	R	V	P	R	I	H	P	J
O	I	P	O	F	L	O	Q	A	I	F	T	M	Y	I	E	P	R	M	U
B	H	Z	O	A	L	K	U	I	V	F	U	P	D	Y	V	W	C	Z	T
G	V	V	R	S	J	B	R	V	O	V	Y	H	B	F	I	G	O	G	E
N	F	Q	F	Y	T	E	Q	P	C	S	G	E	K	N	R	G	E	R	H
I	P	I	R	A	F	A	E	X	Z	H	P	X	A	A	W	R	S	J	K
T	H	L	A	R	W	D	I	P	C	Q	R	A	O	F	J	B	Y	P	E
R	T	Y	M	C	I	I	P	R	Z	H	R	Y	T	Y	P	Y	F	N	N
I	G	H	E	H	N	U	R	W	W	J	N	Y	Z	S	M	K	C	E	B
K	K	B	I	I	D	X	M	I	X	A	V	G	I	T	D	N	C	P	H
S	A	G	D	T	O	O	X	C	N	Z	Y	N	S	I	A	D	M	R	K
Y	L	L	V	R	W	T	P	O	J	G	K	S	K	H	H	F	H	M	I
F	J	D	J	A	S	D	R	X	J	G	N	I	R	E	T	S	A	L	P
T	E	S	M	V	O	B	L	L	A	Z	H	G	C	L	S	W	J	U	N
C	T	U	R	E	M	Z	E	C	V	D	B	M	A	K	K	G	C	D	C
B	W	K	A	R	P	N	G	P	U	A	O	Z	Z	Z	R	B	O	N	S
D	Z	H	D	V	X	M	B	V	Z	D	K	M	P	T	F	S	V	F	Q

1 Find the following words, in the word search above, that are associated with first and second fixings.

- wiring
- pipework
- door frame
- coving
- sink
- bath

- stairways
- taps
- architrave
- windows
- skirting board
- plastering

2   Put these words into the correct category.

First fix	Second fix

- kitchen units

- all wiring

- door frames

- sinks/washing basins/taps

- back boxes for in-house wiring

- plastering

- windows

- floorboards

- pipework

- doors/door ironmongery

- studwork or stud-partitions

- bathroom facilities

- coving/skirting boards

3   In less than 50 words, describe why first fix has to be done before second fix.

_____

_____

_____

_____

_____

_____

_____

4.18   Windows and doors

Student Book
pp 92–93

1   Draw lines to match each type of window with the correct description.

Casement window	Strips of horizontal glass are used to make up the window. These can all be open or shut using a lever. They can be draughty, even when closed, and also the view can be obstructed once they are opened.
Pivot window	Very popular during Victorian times but has recently lost its appeal. There are several styles of this window: square, splayed and curved. They allow you to have a more broad view from the room.
Louvre window	The most popular window, with a large number of styles and sizes available. Are made up of one fixed pane of glass, one side hinged framed pane and a top hung fanlight.
Sash window	These are almost a horizontal version to the sash window. Split in two, the windows slide past one another to provide good ventilation. These windows are usually double-glazed and do not project into the room if opened or shut.
Bay window	Two wooden sashes slide up and down to provide good ventilation. Split in two halves, they can sometimes stick and rattle, and the cords can break. Aluminium versions are now available.
Sliding window	The window can swivel on a pivot and therefore is easy to clean. One pane of glass makes up the entire window and can provide good ventilation, but part of the window, when opened, projects into the room.

2　　Fill in the name of the type of door to match each description.

Door type _____

> The most popular type of internal door. Normally painted to fit into the surrounding environment. They are basic in design but perfectly serviceable.

Door type _____

> These basically consist of two vertical wooden stiles with three horizontal rails. Usually made from softwood for internal use and hardwood for external, they are more aesthetically pleasing than the previous type of doors.

Door type _____

> A strong door that is normally associated with cottages. A simple door that is made up of tongue and groove boards. The best type of boarded door is the framed, ledged and braced door.

Door type _____

> A wooden frame holds a number of wooden slats which are set at an angle. Air can pass freely through these slats and so this type of door is normally used for cupboards.

Door type _____

> The frame is usually made from aluminium although plastic and wood can also be used. These are used to bring the living room and garden together as they are fully glazed from floor to ceiling.

3　Take a tour of your house or school and find examples of the windows and doors that are mentioned above. Make a list of what you find and where each type is used.

4　Draw sketches of three of the examples of windows or doors named above, labelling their features.

4.19   External works, drainage and landscaping

1   Fill in the advantages and disadvantages of the systems listed in the table below.

Drainage	Advantages	Disadvantages
Combined system		
Totally separate system		
Partially separate system		

2   Label the partially separate drainage system.

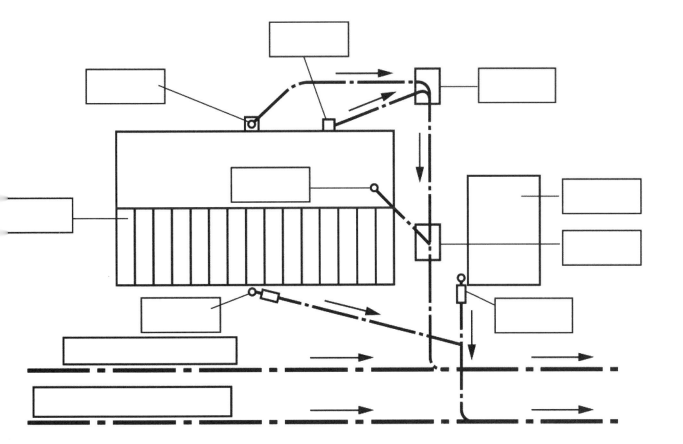

3   Complete the diagram below with as many different types of external works as possible.

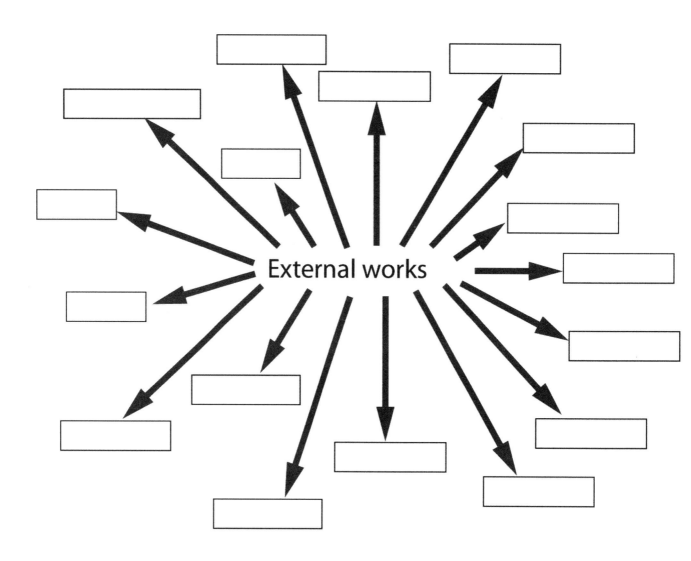

4.20   Demolition

Student Book
pp 96–97

Demolition is an important sustainable issue for construction projects. The recycling of demolished buildings into re-useable fill material is important in saving finite resources.

1   Identify two uses of sustainable demolition products.

_____

_____

_____

_____

_____

_____

_____

_____

_____

2   List three advantages of retaining as much demolition materials on site for the wider community as a whole.

_____

_____

_____

_____

_____

_____

_____

_____

4.21   Construction plant: Details and application

Student Book
pp 98–99

1 Identify from the following list those items of plant that have *wheels*, those that have *tracks* and the one item that has *neither*.

- JCB 3CX
- tower crane
- dumper truck
- 360° excavator

- forklift truck
- crane
- concrete pump

2 You are working as an assistant site manager. You have been asked to order an excavator for the construction site. What factors do you need to carefully consider when ordering this piece of plant? For example, you may need to think about the volume of the excavation required. List five more factors.

3 Fill in the missing words.

The old Wembley Stadium was taken down quickly using _____ plant and equipment. The new Wembley Stadium was built on foundations that used _____ to dig them, concrete _____ to pour the foundations and structure, and _____ to erect the frame and the famous arch. A wide range of construction plant made this job _____ and _____.

easy   cranes   pumps   demolition   quick   excavators

4.22   Site management

**Student Book
pp 100–101**

1   From the following list, circle the personnel who are normally involved in site management (as opposed to being in Head Office).

- planner
- estimator
- contract supervisor
- general foreperson
- managing director

- general operative
- joiner
- quantity surveyor
- bricklayer
- buyer

2   Draw lines to match each operative name with the correct type of work.

bricklayer	setting out
joiner	supervising
general operative	moving materials
ground-worker	laying bricks
site manager	laying drainage
site engineer	nailing roof timbers

3   You have just joined a company as assistant contracts manager. The human resources manager has approached you to help recruit some site personnel. You have been tasked with producing a job description for a site manager. This should contain a list of the roles and responsibilities that the postholder will undertake on site.

Produce such a brief description to be used in an advert in a large national newspaper. The advert will fill half a page. Make your main points in a series of five or so headings, each with bullet points underneath giving more detail. For example, one such heading might be 'Health and safety responsibilities' followed by several bullet points outlining specific health and safety duties.

4.23 Organisation and programming

**Student Book
pp 102–103**

1   Which of the items in the following list would the planner in a construction company undertake? Who would undertake the remaining ones?

■ Work out the price for labour

■ Produce a master programme

■ Undertake a health and safety audit on site

■ Schedule delivery dates

■ Plan the layout of the site

■ Organise site labour

■ Monitor progress on site

2   The site manager now has to plan for the labour requirements on site and has given you a list of how many operatives are required for each activity.

Using the gantt chart below, place each of these labour requirements onto the bar chart activities for each day that the activity lasts. When your gantt chart is complete, calculate the total labour requirements for each day.

Labour numbers per day

Cast base for garage	2	Window and door	2
Brick walls	5	Electrics	5
Roof installation	4	Painting	3
Roof covering	3		

	Cast base for garage	Brick walls	Roof installation	Roof covering	Window and door	Electrics	Painting
16							
15							
14							
13							
12							
11							
10							
9							
8							
7							
6							
5							
4							
3							
2							
1							
Days							

3   Imagine the following delays have occurred. Recalculate the gantt chart to show a revised completion date.

■ Roof covering now three days

■ Brick walls overrun by five days

4.24 Information technology in project management

**Student Book
pp 104–105**

1 Identify from the following list (the left-hand side) which are ICT applications that might be used on a construction project, then match the correct description against each item by drawing an arrow

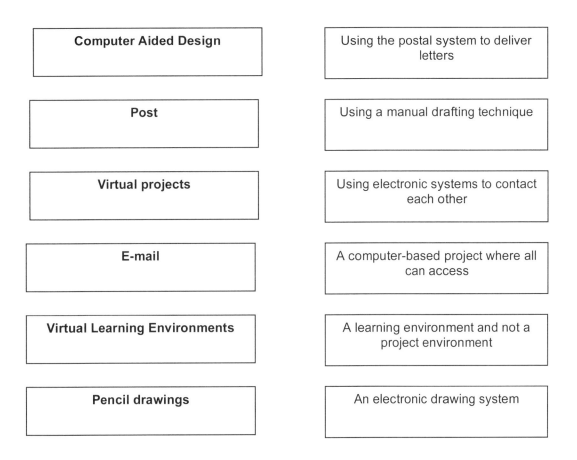

Computer Aided Design		Using the postal system to deliver letters
Post		Using a manual drafting technique
Virtual projects		Using electronic systems to contact each other
E-mail		A computer-based project where all can access
Virtual Learning Environments		A learning environment and not a project environment
Pencil drawings		An electronic drawing system

2 The following is a small Gantt chart for a short project. Have a detailed look at it and decide in teams how you would go about drawing such a chart. List the steps you would take in a checklist for another person to use.

Time	1	2	3	4	5	6	7	8	9	10	11	12	13
Excavation	■	■											
Concrete		■	■	■									
Brickwork				■	■	■	■						
Steelwork							■	■					
Roof								■	■	■			
Interior walls										■	■		
Car park											■	■	
Handover													■

4.25   Sustainable site practice 1: Community issues

Student Book
pp 106–107

1   Using information from the website <u>www.ccscheme.org.uk</u>, create a presentation on how to be a considerate constructor. Extend your work by investigating further to find images of construction taking place in a considerate manner.

2   Imagine that you are a technical assistant of a construction company. You have been asked by a local journalist to explain how the company takes into consideration the views of the local community. Write a report outlining how you think your company should do this.

4.26   Sustainable site practice 2: Environmental issues

**Student Book
pp 108–109**

1   Using the internet, books or other resources, identify the following terms and write a definition for them.

Key term	Definition
Fossil fuel	
Greenhouse gases	
Bund wall	
Silt trap	
Embodied energy	

2   Read this paragraph on embodied energy and fill in the gaps.

These days it is not appropriate to just consider the energy used by a _____ throughout its life. Indeed, the improvements in insulation standards and appliance efficiency mean that the _____ consumed in the production of materials and the _____ of a building have a much greater significance than ever before. Embodied energy is the _____ energy consumed in the production of a _____. The diagram below shows all the sources of embodied _____ within a project. This includes the energy consumed during the extraction and _____ of raw materials, off-site manufacturing of components, site construction and _____ at all stages.

energy   transportation   building   energy   building
total   construction   processing

5

Create the Built Environment: Using Tools

Unit overview

Health and Safety is an important topic that must be considered in all practical situations that a student becomes involved within. In this unit the student will undertake a practical exercise, producing some work to the pathway they are following.

Careful consideration must be given to the hazards and risks involved. This has been woven into a learning outcome for this unit. Personal protective equipment has to be selected and used correctly and appropriately for each pathway. Safe systems of work and practices must be followed. Good housekeeping is essential in this unit, for maintaining a clean and tidy working environment.

The second learning outcome asks the student to understand the working characteristics and safe use of materials for a straight forward task. For example, the safe handling of bricks on site, where weight and manual handling must be taken into account.

Following this the student is then set two tasks within the unit. The first is a practical task in their chosen pathway of brickwork, carpentry and joinery, building services or painting and decorating. The second task covers a presentation by the student to their peer group on job roles and responsibilities. Here there is an opportunity for functional skills in English in speaking and listening and presentations skills using ICT.

The practical tasks involve working to tolerances and as such the students have to build up a certain skill level to achieve this standard using hand and power tools where appropriate. The student has to calculate quantities, cutting lists and other sizes and volumes and here clear links exist to functional skills. The student has to self check their work against these tolerances, commenting on its quality and performance.

Links with other units

Level 1
- Unit 3: Create the built environment: Using tools
- Unit 4: Create the built environment: Methods and materials

114 © Owned by or under licence to Pearson Education Limited 2008.

Topics covered	Edexcel unit learning outcomes
Health and safety legislation	Know about, use and be able to extend own implementation of health and safety practices in a construction craft environment
Personal protective equipment and materials	Understand the working characteristics and safe use of materials
Tools and equipment	Be able to use tools safely and effectively to produce a practical outcome
Brickwork, Carpentry and Joinery, Painting and Decorating, Building Services	Understand the job roles, progression routes, occupational structures and importance of teamwork in the crafts and related activities

How this unit will be assessed

Assessment is based on the student being able to demonstrate that they have met four areas of learning outcomes. These are:

LO 5.1 Know about, use and be able to extend own implementation of health and safety practices in a construction craft environment
LO 5.2 Understand the working characteristics and safe use of materials
LO 5.3 Be able to use tools safely and effectively to produce a practical outcome
LO 5.4 Understand the job roles, progression routes, occupational structures and importance of teamwork in the crafts and related activities

Marks are awarded across three banded levels with an increasing amount of evidence required to meet the higher band three outcomes. These are clearly specified in the assessment marking table within the specification.

Marks are awarded based upon the depth of knowledge a student demonstrates in each of the focus areas. This means they could theoretically achieve top marks in one assessment focus and a score of nil in another. Assessment foci are marked in three bands: band 1 generally asks the student to 'briefly describe' or 'evaluate', band 2 asks for 'descriptions', band 3 asks for 'explanation and justification'. Assessment should be based on a 'best fit' approach to the grid.

This assessment is divided into two tasks that are activity based which cover the two learning outcomes as follows. The student must produce a written report in A4 word processed format. Any drawings should be smaller than A3 size. Each page of the portfolio should be numbered and include your name.

Learning Outcome 5.1: Know about, use and be able to extend own implementation of health and safety practices in a construction craft environment; Learning Outcome 5.2: Understand the working characteristics and safe use of materials; Learning Outcome 5.3: Be able to use tools safely and effectively to produce a practical outcome

This task is practically based within a workshop environment. The student should be given an induction into workshop safety before commencing the task. This task is split into the chosen pathways of brickwork, carpentry and joinery, building services, and painting and decorating. The following are the requirements for each skill area.

Brickwork

The student has to produce one meter square of half brick wall in stretcher bond with a bucket handle pointed joint one side. Variety can be introduced by using different coloured bricks within the panel for differentiation.

Carpentry and Joinery

The student has a choice of two test models to construct.

Model 1

The student has to construct a timber planter from prepared materials using supplied fixings. The planter has an open top of area $0.2m^2$ and a height of 300mm. It can be square or rectangular with solid sides. The base needs to be raised off the floor by 75mm. All components should be connected using suitable jointing methods.

Model 2

The student has to manufacture a frame ledged and braced door with v-jointed match boarding using prepared materials. The door can be full or half size and constructed using appropriate jointing methods. The student will need to fit a mortise deadlock with escutcheon plates.

Painting and Decorating

The student has to complete three tasks within this skill area.

Task 1

A complete decoration of a bay area to include a section of emulsioned wall, a ceiling area, skirting boards, electrical sockets and a window or door frame. All surfaces are to be prepared properly and all cutting in is to be completed.

Task 2

To prepare and wall paper a section of wall which includes trimming to ceiling, skirting boards, sockets and a window or door frame.

Task 3

To fully prepare and paint a flush door or casement window using a gloss finish.

Building Services

The student has to complete two tasks within this skill area.

Task 1

Using mounting boards the leaner has to complete the wiring of a consumer unit with five ring main socket outlets and two spur socket outlets. A lighting circuit with two one way switched lights and one two way switched light is also to be included.

Task 2

The student must complete a 15mm copper pipework installation. This is to incorporate a 15mm stop tap or isolating valve, a bib tap, two compression t fittings (one manipulative one not), one soldered t joint, three soldered elbow fittings, two end caps, and a minimum of 2300mm of pipework. The student must water test the system when complete.

What guidance will you give?

The student should be encouraged to plan the task methodically. The use of high quality digital photographs is essential to record both progress and evidence as the task proceeds. There are two learning outcomes that include health and safety issues on the identification of hazards associated with the work, the use of PPE and COSHH. The student could cover some of these within a formal risk assessment format. The student is encouraged to take responsibility for their own working environment, ensuring it is hazard free and is clean and tidy.

What should you look for in marking?

The student needs to identify the principal hazards associated with the practical task, including those associated with the materials used. The persons at risk need establishing. The student needs to demonstrate safe working practices, the correct use of PPE and the correct application of the COSHH regulations to any substances used. A reflection element in what they have learnt needs to conclude the completion of the practical task.

The materials used in producing the various models need to be described along with any site procedures associated with safe working practices. The student must demonstrate reasonable skills in producing the practical element of this learning outcome. This includes some self checking on quality control.

What gains higher assessment marks?

The student needs to describe clearly all of the hazards and risks associated with the practical element, whilst independently demonstrating consistent safe working practices. The COSHH element must be justified. Reflection in what skills the student has developed must be clearly described.

The use of alternative materials and their advantages and disadvantages has to be explored with a clear site evaluation on their use.

A higher level of practical skills must be demonstrated by detailed and accurate quality manufacture of the task.

How could students present the evidence?

Evidence should be presented within a technical report. This can contain witness statements, observation records, photographs, descriptions, and health and safety documents. The format should be clearly laid out and presented for assessment.

Learning Outcome 5.4: Understand the job roles, progression routes, occupational structures and importance of teamwork in the crafts and related activities

This task covers a team presentation where the student can demonstrate their knowledge on the key job roles, responsibilities and qualifications associated with construction. These are at craft, technical, supervisory and management levels.

The amount of detail on each role for this description should contain: title, purpose, nature of work, interactions, teamwork, skills, experience, qualifications required, career progression and the role of professional institutions.

Working as an individual the student must take part in the team presentation, by contributing to the planning of the presentation materials. The student will have to take part in a discussion on the presentation of two job roles.

What guidance will you give?

The student will need to develop some presentation skills in order to be able to discuss this task in front of their peers. Time should be given to prepare and practice for this role within a team. Team selection should also be carefully considered in personalities and individual requirements.

What should you look for in marking?

Two different craft job roles must be presented and discussed including progression routes, teamwork and the roles of any associated professional bodies.

What gains higher assessment marks?

The description of the craft roles must be extended to include supervisory, technical and professional roles. The interaction and teamwork aspects between roles needs to be included. The role of the relevant professional body must be justified in a description.

How could students present the evidence?

Evidence must be included in the format of a portfolio. This could contain developed PowerPoint slides, planning notes, video recording of presentation, transcripts, question and answer sheet.

Delivering this unit

This unit will require the use of a practical workshop. Here the students can identify hazards and risks associated with producing their practical models in their chosen pathway. Drawings will have to be produced for the student to follow when building the practical assessment. Tolerances need to be built into these drawings.

The information in the student book for this unit is written in topics, each topic covering a particular learning outcome that relates to the awarding bodies specification. There are tasks at the end of each topic, some of which can be used to help with the production of the reports that have to be completed for this unit.

The activities in the ADR will reinforce students knowledge and can also be used to help build up evidence for the report.

Several of the activities are to reinforce knowledge learned in the student book and can be used to check understanding and be used as revision tools throughout this unit.

Integrating Functional Skills

Functional Skills can be applied throughout the topic both in the SB and the activities.

English – students will demonstrate their use of English throughout all the activities.

Speaking and listening – by contributing to discussions and making presentations and asking questions of outside speakers.

Reading – reading and understanding texts and using them to research and gather information.

Writing – communicating with others by using various written methods such as reports and letters.

ICT – students should be able to use ICT independently for a variety of tasks. They should be able to communicate and exchange information safely and responsibly, use the Internet for research and be able to present information in an effective and appropriate way such as producing text, images, tables, graphs and diagrams.

Personal, Learning and Thinking Skills

Some embedded uses of PLTS are incorporated in certain Edexcel assessment activities (see QCF unit summary inside the Edexcel unit specifications). However, use should be made of all opportunities to develop and enhance each students PLTS. Suitable opportunities will arise during the delivery and assessment activities for all of the elements of the Diploma. For example, the student may use their work experience to add to their PLTS experience and engagement. The development of the evidence portfolio on design will give the student the opportunity to use their personal and thinking skills in the solutions.

Linking to the Project

Some of the activities can be used as part of the students' project or can be the starting point towards gaining knowledge and information that will be developed should they wish to pursue this topic for their project. The relevant activities will point this out on the page.

Other useful resources

Work experience will further learning and understanding of how the sectors and services work together and these experiences will also aid work on the reports. In some circumstances this may be difficult to arrange therefore valuable insights can be obtained and primary evidence collected by inviting professionals in the sectors or services to visit and talk to the students as they can provide a stimulating input and enhance the learning of students.

Students should be encouraged to work in pairs or groups to gather information although they **must be aware** that they will need to produce an **individual report and project**.

Useful websites

- www.hse.gov.uk
- www.hse.gov.uk/coshh
- www.coshh-essentials.org.uk
- www.architecture.com/
- www.ciat.org.uk/

- www.rics.org
- www.cibse.org
- www.ice.org.uk
- www.ciob.org.uk

Scheme of work

Insert Centre
Logo Here

Title:

Centre Name:

Level 2 Diploma in Construction and the Built Environment

Unit 5 Create the built environment: Using tools

Academic year: ....

Edexcel unit learning outcome: Know about, use and be able to extend own implementation of health and safety practices in a construction craft environment

Understand the working characteristics and safe use of materials

Be able to use tools safely and effectively to produce a practical outcome

Understand the job roles, progression routes, occupational structures and importance of teamwork in the crafts and related activities

This scheme of work provides information for all four craft area options. Students only need to address one of these options, not all four.

Tutor/Lecturer(s).........................   **Guided learning hours: 60 GLH (45 + 15)**

SB = Student Book

ADR = Assessment and Delivery Resource

GLH	Outcome/topic	Content	Student activity	Resources	Link to Learning objective
All students					
4.5	Health and safety legislation	• Why we need health and safety legislation • The difference between hazards and risks • What a risk assessment is • Who is at risk?	• Write down thoughts on why we need legislation • Record the different types of legislation • Join tutor discussion on what they are, who they protect and what hazards are present on site • Complete an exemplar of a risk assessment • Students produce a poster on site hazards and draw up a set of rules	• Activities 1, 2 SB p115 • ADR activities p137 • Computer with internet access	LO.5.1/1 LO.5.1/2
3	Personal protective equipment	• Where PPE should be worn • Essential PPE	• Students to discuss what hazards PPE might be required for	• Activity 1,2, 3 SB 117	LO.5.1/3

		Content	Activities	Resources	LO
	(PPE)	• Whose responsibility is PPE? • COSHH PPE requirements	• Look at different types of PPE, how they are used/worn and for what reason • Students to create a leaflet highlighting PPE	• Case study SB p117 • ADR activities p138	
3	**Access equipment**	• The main factors to consider when choosing access equipment • Appropriate site access procedures • Using a ladder • Safety when working at height	• Students list types of access equipment and consider in a tutor-led discussion • Students to research case study on access equipment on site, covering safety checks and equipment types	• Starter activity SB p118 • Case study SB p119 • Computer suite • ADR activities p139	LO.5.2/1
4.5	**Assessment Sessions**	• Students undertake the first session of assessment	• Learning Objective LO.5.1	• Assessment portfolio/ assignment task sheet	LO.5.1
Craft area option 1: Brickwork					
3	**Brickwork 1 – bricks and blocks**	• The different types of bricks available for different uses • Special types of bricks • Working characteristics of bricks • Blocks • The safe use of brickwork	• Students work in pairs to define the differences between a brick and a block? • Learn what bricks are and work out the modular length of a brick wall • Learn what blocks are and work out the modular length of a block wall • Students design a freestanding wall	• Starter activity SB p120 • Activities 1, 2, 3 SB p121 • ADR activities p140–1	LO.5.2
3	**Brickwork 2 – sundry materials**	The sundry materials used in the construction of a build: • DPC • Wall ties • Mortars • Lintels • Cavity wall insulation	• Students to observe a house and report on what has been used other than bricks • Tutor-led discussion on the main areas of sundry materials • Internet- or library-based research on wall ties	• Internet access • Activities 1, 2, 3 SB p123 • ADR Activities p142	LO.5.2

Hours	Topic	Content	Activities	Resources	LO
3	Brickwork 3 – tools	• The tools you will need to complete your assessed practical task • The correct tools to use when accurately cutting bricks	• Investigate and explore tools to be used in project • Practical experience of individual tools, identifying and using equipment • Produce a leaflet that promotes safety onsite • Students role-play a bricklayer scenarios on designing and constructing walls	• All tools needed to complete practical project • Activity 1, 2, 3 SB p124 • For your project SB p124 • ADR activities p143, p172	LO.5.3
3	Brickwork 4 – brickwork bonds	• Three brickwork bonds • Bonds which use headers to tie the two skins of brickwork together • How bonding helps to spread the load of the structure	• Students to investigate the different types of brickwork bonds and tour school or college to identify different types of brickwork bonds used • Produce a sketch of an English or Flemish bond and label this, stating differences between these and the other bonds • Complete a table describing the three main types of bond	• Activities 1, 2, 3 SB p126 • For you project p126 • ADR activities p144	LO.5.2
6	Brickwork 5 – laying bricks to line	• What the major function of the brickwork bed joint is • How a line should be set up and used • Why bricklayers work from three different packs of bricks • Using skills to produce brickwork	• Students to consider the nature of a brickwork joint before a tutor-led discussion and demonstration of the process of laying bricks • Students attempt their own brick laying • Students produce a step-by-step guide to cover the main methods and investigate brick sizes using this to form a PowerPoint presentation • Investigate the best way bricks can be produced and consider health and safety	• Starter activity p128 • Activities 1, 2, 3 SB p128 • ADR activities p145	LO.5.3
3	Brickwork 6 – jointing and quality control	• Different brickwork joints • Recording quality control checks in your project work • Why newly laid brickwork has to be protected	• Students consider the look of different buildings and suggest why some look better than others • Observe and discuss different joints • Study exemplars of how to record quality control checks in own project work • Produce a poster that explains advantages and disadvantages of different methods • Complete tables in ADR activities	• Activities 1, 2, 3 SB p131 • For your project p130 • ADR activities p146–7	LO.5.3
6	Assessment Sessions	• Students undertake the second session of assessment	• Learning Objective LO.5.2/5.3	• Assessment portfolio/ assignment task sheet	LO 5.2/5.3

Craft area option 2: Carpentry and joinery

Hours	Topic	Content	Activities	Resources	LO
3	Carpentry and	• Different hand tools that a carpenter	• Students to identify different tools including	• Activities 1, 2 SB p133	LO.5.2

Hours	Topic	Learning content	Teaching and learning activities	Resources	LO
	joinery 1 – hand tools and equipment	power tools • The advantages of using power tools • Health and safety associated with these tools	• Students to mark out a dovetail joint • Students to work in groups to create a safety document for using a circular saw • Students create a series of sketches based around health and safety • Students create mortice and tenon joint	• Personal learning and thinking skills SB p133 • Functional skills SB p133 • ADR activities p148, p173	LO.5.3
3	**Carpentry and joinery 2 – softwoods and hardwoods**	• The main differences between softwoods and hardwoods • Woods which are best suited to outdoor use • Factors in choosing wood, apart from the purpose	• Students research three advantages and disadvantages of softwoods and hardwoods • Identify different softwoods • Identify different hardwoods • Investigate origins of different woods and why there are so many types of hardwood	• Activities 1, 2 SB p135 • ADR activities p149–50	LO.5.2
3	**Carpentry and joinery 3 – manufactured boards**	• The main types of manufactured board • Why manufactured boards are popular in the modern construction industry • Manufactured boards and sustainability	• Tutor-led discussion on why manufactured boards are used over hardwoods/softwoods • Look at examples of manufactured boards • Discuss advantages and disadvantages, with students investigating how they are manufactured and costs • Draw a 3-D shell of a house showing areas where manufactured boards would be used	• Activities 1, 2 SB p137 • Functional skills SB p138 • ADR activities p151–2	LO.5.2
3	**Carpentry and joinery 4 – miscellaneous materials**	• What miscellaneous means • The broad categories of materials that come under the 'miscellaneous' umbrella • How miscellaneous materials can make a job quicker or better	• Students complete a mind-map in group discussion of miscellaneous materials • Observe different miscellaneous materials – students to identify what they are for, how they work, adhesives and fixings • Students to identify why these materials are important in construction and identify examples in the classroom	• Starter activity SB p138 • Activities 1, 2, 3 SB p138 • ADR activities p153	LO.5.2

	Topic	Content	Resources / Activities	LO
3	**Carpentry and joinery 5 – quality control**	• What the purpose of quality control is and what records need keeping • How conversion and seasoning affects the way wood reacts to its environment • The tests that can be done to determine whether the material is best for a job	• Students discuss in pairs the possible impact of no quality control in the industry • Join tutor-led discussion on conversion and seasoning and quality control • Students research and identify visual checks and importance of experience • Students prepare a report on 'dry assemble' joints • Students research and describe conversion methods	• Activities 1, 2, 3 SB p140 • ADR activities p154	LO.5.2
3	**Carpentry and joinery 6 – efficient use of resources**	• Why materials need to be transported and stored correctly • The impact that correct use of materials has on waste • What benefits come from the efficient use of resources?	• Students to list ways that you could look after materials when in storage as part of tutor-led discussion on the efficient use and storage of resources • Students role-play training new recruits in a materials store • Students research how best to transport and store key materials and role-play resolving a customer complaint on damaged goods	• Start activity SB p142 • Activities 1, 2, 3 SB p143 • ADR activities p155	LO.5.2
3	**Carpentry and joinery 7 – wood joints**	• What the purposes of wood joints are • The main types of wood joint • Health and safety considerations when preparing wood joints • Use appropriate skills to produce a practical task • Health and safety considerations	• Students write down thoughts on why there are different types of wood joint • Discussion and research on different wood joints and how and why they are used • Students draw own diagrams of planter and wood joints in a gate • Research and describe three advantages and disadvantages of CADCAM • Students to select a joint to create	• Starter activity p144 • Activities 1, 2, 3 SB p145 • ADR activities p156–7	LO.5.2
6	**Assessment Sessions**	• Students undertake the second session of assessment	• Learning Objective LO.5.2/5.3	• Assessment portfolio/assignment task sheet	LO 5.2/5.3
Craft area option 3: Painting and decorating				
3	**Painting and decorating 1 – decoration**	• Decoration in a room • Use of colour • Use of texture	• Students to consider how a room in their home could be decorated and prepare a proposal for doing so, drawing up a plan • Students to study restaurant decorating case study and suggest materials and designs that would fit the situation described	• Start activity SB p146 • Case study SB p147 • ADR activities p158	LO 5.2

	Topic	Content	Activities	Resources	LO
3	**Painting and decorating 2 – tools and equipment**	• Different tools for different finishes • Quality control	• Students to observe and familiarise selves with specialist tools used for painting and decorating • Students to research case study, describing what the scenario would require • Students to complete table identifying tools	• Starter activity SB p148 • Case study SB p148 • ADR activities p159–60, p175	LO.5.2
6	**Painting and decorating 3 – materials**	• Differences between preparatory wallpaper and a finish paper • Surface preparation materials • Paints, varnishes, glazes and stains	• Students to consider materials used for painting as stimulus for tutor-led discussion • General discussion on surface preparation materials, paints, varnishes, glazes and stains • Observe different wallpapers and pastes • Students to research case study, describing what the scenario would require • Students to prepare a written report on the advantages and disadvantages of products • Students to perform test calculation for dimensions when painting	• Starter activity SB p150 • Functional skills p150 • Case study SB p150 • ADR activities p161	LO.5.2
3	**Painting and decorating 4 – painting**	• What are the reasons for painting? • What is an unsound surface? • What methods of application are there? • The need for good preparation before painting	• Tutor-led discussion on the four reasons for painting – what do they mean? • Tutor-led discussion of surface preparation, paint systems and application methods • Students to research case study, describing what the scenario would require • Students to research in what scenarios certain types of paint would be used	• Starter activity SB p152 • Case study SB p152 • ADR activities p162	LO.5.2
3	**Painting and decorating 5 – wallpapering**	• Types of paper • Wallpaper symbols • Preparation • Skills required to produce quality work	• Students to guess the use of different papers, and record their answers • Tutor-led discussion of different types of papers and their uses and information session on wallpaper symbols • Students to research case study, describing what the scenario would require • Complete calculations for requirements for painting and decorating a room	• Starter activity SB p154 • Case study SB p155 • ADR activities p163	LO.5.2

	Topic	Content	Delivery/Activities	Resources	LO
3	**Painting and decorating 6 – quality control and common defects**	• Surface defects • Paint film defects • Treatments • Quality control records	• Tutor-led discussion and observation of different surface defects • Look at examples of paint film defects and discussion on preventative methods • Tutor-led discussion on defects of coverings • Students to research case study, describing what the scenario would require • Students to work in pairs to produce a brief report on probable causes of common defects	• Starter activity SB p156 • Case study SB p157 • ADR activities p164	LO.5.2
6	**Assessment Sessions**	• Students undertake the second session of assessment	• Learning Objective LO.5.2/5.3	• Assessment portfolio/ assignment task sheet	LO 5.2/5.3
Craft area option 4: Building services					
3	**Building services 1 – tools and equipment**	• Tools and equipment used by plumbers and electricians • The right tool for the work or task • Health and safety with tools	• Students to list tools and equipment needed before reading on • Observe and use unfamiliar tools and equipment • Students to research case study, describing what the scenario would require • Students create safety leaflet for power tools and investigate unfamiliar tools further • Students to research selected tools and find out more on use and cost	• Starter activity SB p158 • Case study SB p159 • Activities 1, 2 and 3 SB p159 • ADR activities p165–6, p176	LO.5.2
4.5	**Building services 2 – materials (plumbing)**	• Properties of materials • Pipework – plastic and metals • Site procedures with using materials	• Research and discussion on why lead has been replaced by plastics and copper • Learn about properties of materials through tutor-led examples and discussion • Students to collect examples of materials and their uses	• Starter activity SB p160 • Activities 1, 2 and 3 SB p160 • ADR activities p167	LO.5.2
4.5	**Building services 3 – materials (electrical)**	• Electrical materials • Cable • Components	• Students to investigate the role of an electrician and prepare mini-report • Observe and discuss different types of cable and components • Students to collect examples of cable • Students to sketch a possible design for a consumer unit and label it fully	• Starter activity SB p162 • Activities 1, 2 and 3 SB p162 • ADR activities p168	LO.5.2

Hours	Topic	Content	Resources	LO
4.5	**Building services 4 – jointing methods**	• Jointing methods for plumbing and electrical work • Practical skills required to produce joints	• Students estimate number of joints in a plumbing system and an electrical system in a house • Tutor-led demonstration of jointing methods for plumbing and electrical work • Locate images of brass fittings and collect a file, comparing items in terms of cost, function and appearance • Inspect two different sockets and describe how to terminate a cable in each	• Starter activity SB p164 • Activities 1, 2 and 3 SB p164 • ADR activities p169–70	LO.5.2
3	**Building services 5 – quality control and common defects**	• Quality control in plumbing and electrical work • Common defects in plumbing and electrical work	• Students to define quality control and check definition before observing poor work • Join tutor-led discussion on quality control and common defects • Students work in pairs to practice connecting a conductor to a terminal and making a compression joint	• Starter activity SB p166 • Activities 1, 2, 3 SB p166 • ADR activities p171	LO.5.2
6	**Assessment Sessions**	• Students undertake the forth session of assessment	• Learning Objective LO.5.2/5.3	• Assessment portfolio/ assignment task sheet	LO 5.2/5.3
All students				
4.5	**Job roles and responsibilities – the construction team**	• Different job roles within the construction industry • Collaboration within the team • Teamwork and interaction	• Students create a mind-map of different jobs available in the construction industry • Feedback and discussion on job roles • Research specific job roles and institutions	• Starter activity SB p112 • Activity 1, 2 SB p113 • ADR activities p135–6 • Internet access	LO.5.4
3	**Progression pathways**	• Progression from craft to supervisor • Progression into a professional role • Introduction to the professional institutions	Students to conduct research into: • Health and safety procedures • Working characteristics of materials • Job roles within this area	• Internet access • Access to computer and power point • List of useful websites	LO.5.4
3	**Professional Institutions**	• The role of the professional institutions • Qualifications and training • Link to unit 3	• Investigate further the professional institutions identified in Unit 3 • Web based research into Institutions	• ICT, computer and projector • Note-taking grid	LO.5.4
3	**Understanding job roles within this area**	• Guidance on this section • Preparation for assessment	• Make notes on this section • Write this section of the report for assessment	• Mark scheme • Computer access • Internet access	LO.5.4
4.5	**Assessment Sessions**	• Students undertake the fifth session of assessment	• Learning Objective LO.5.2/5.3/5.4	• Assessment portfolio/ assignment task sheet	LO 5.2/5.3/5.4

Level 2 Diploma in Construction and the Built Environment

Lesson plan 1 (craft area option 1)
Unit 5: Create the built environment: Using Tools – Brickwork

Centre name: · Tutor/lecturer(s):

Aims & objectives

- Learn to demonstrate the safe and correct use of the tools appropriate to the task
- Maintain a tidy working area and clean area once task is completed
- Handle tools with appropriate care and clean after use

SB = Student Book
ADR = Assessment and Delivery Resource

Learning objectives

- Know about health and safety procedures in a construction craft environment LO.5.1/1
- Understand the safe working characteristics and safe use of materials LO.5.2/1
- Be able to use tools safely and effectively to produce a practical outcome LO.5.3/1

NB. Some centres may need to work with an external provider of training in order to enable students to practice and apply the vocational skills to enable them to complete the task.

Timings reflect one typical session within the GLH block of 3 hours allocated in the SOW

Total lesson time: 120 minutes

Timing/ Content	Teacher activity	Student activity	Resources	Individualised activity/differentiation	Personal learning and thinking skills	Functional skills
5 mins Register	Check health and safety of the room Take a register	Enter room in accordance with normal procedures and settle	Register			
5 mins Starter	Introduce starter: SB p124 Get practical! – write down the tools and PPE that you think you will need to complete your practical task.	Students work in pairs to think about the different tools and PPE they will need to complete their practical project	SB page 124	Quick fire, feedback to teacher – prompting by the tutor	Effective participators Teamwork	

Time / Topic	Teacher activity	Student activity	Resources	Support / Differentiation	PLTS	Functional skills (English)
5 mins Identification of materials and tools	Remind students what the practical element of the project involves. Show the selection of materials they will get during the lesson	Students identify the materials they will use during lesson				
5 mins Collection of tools and equipment	Allow Students time in which to try and identify the tools and equipment needed to set up working area	Students to set up their working area with all tools, materials and equipment	Sand and lime mortar, Brick trowels, Spot boards, Spot board stands, Bucket and brush, Appropriate PPE — Tools ready for Students to select, brick trowels, spot board and stands, bucket and brush, appropriate PPE	Identification and selection of appropriate tools for the task.	Self awareness	
5 mins	Information given to students on why mortar is usually mixed with cement on sites, why lime is added to make it more workable and they will be using sand and lime mix as this will not permanently set the bricks.	Students listening, answering questions. Why is this important for your project work practice?	Mortar and storage area			English skills – Students to improve their questioning and analysis of information
5 mins Demo	Demonstration of rolling mortar – remind students of need to wet spot board so that the wood doesn't leach the water out of mortar. Q&A of important points	Students to watch demonstration and answer questions	Working area reflective of student spaces in order to demonstrate the technique of preparing mortar for spreading	Select student(s) to have a go in front of peers – important to gain confidence	Teamwork – students to create samples	
5 mins	Supervision of the collection of Mortar	Collection of mortar for rolling	Mortar – sand and lime mix	Support for students who need it		
30 mins	Supervision of students beginning to roll mortar	Practicing rolling mortar	Mortar, tools and equipment	One to one demonstrations if needed		
10 mins (demo) **30 mins** Student activity	Important to ensure all students can master - time is needed and reinforcement of the skill – would be useful to demonstrate to students again to point out common mistakes and offer praise	Students to watch demonstration again, to ask any questions and flag up any difficulties they are having with the task. Then continue with task				English skills – Students to improve their questioning and analysis of information
5 mins Plenary	Plenary – Q and A on mortar mixes, why lime is used, why in school/college sand and lime is used, tool and equipment names, task order	Listening, answering questions – completion of ADR for homework	ADR – brickwork practical activity p172			Students use Q&A session to develop English skills
10 mins	Explanation and supervision over how to clean down working area	Cleaning work area on completion of the task	Brushes, area for used mortar, storage area for equipment			

Level 2 Diploma in Construction and the Built Environment

Lesson plan 2 (craft area option 2)

Unit 5: Create the built environment: Using tools – Carpentry and Joinery

Centre name:

Tutor/lecturer(s):

Aims & objectives

- To consider manufacture of a through Mortice and Tenon joint.

SB = Student Book 1
ADR = Assessment and Delivery Resource

Learning objectives

- All students should understand what a mortice and tenon joint is LO.5.3
- Most should be able to identify the correct tools and manufacturing processes to successfully manufacture the wood joint LO.5.3

Timings reflect one typical session within the GLH block of 3 hours allocated in the SOW

Total lesson time: 90 minutes

Timing/ Content	Tutor activity	Student activity	Resources	Individualised activity/differentiation	Personal Learning and Thinking Skills	Functional Skills
5 mins Welcome students and Register	Check health and safety of the room. Take a register	Enter room in accordance with normal procedures and settle quickly	Register			
10 mins Starter	Tutor to give introduction to the manufacture of the mortice and tenon joint and why it is used	Students to listen and take notes on Tutors explanation	Examples of joints	Discussion with Q&A session on wood joints and why they are used		Class discussion and Q&A to develop debating skills
10 mins	Tutor to explain the correct way in which a mortice and tenon joint is marked out	Write down clear notes with diagrams that explain how the wood joint is marked out	Whiteboard + projector ADR p173	Direction for weaker students to clearly draw and annotate the mortice and tenon joint		

Time / Topic	Tutor activity	Student activity	Resources	More able	Additional
20 mins Functional skills Marking out of wood joint	Tutor to demonstrate to students how the mortice and tenon joint is marked out on timber in the workshop	Students to watch demonstration to clearly visualise how to mark out the mortice and tenon wood joint	Timber, set square, marking gauge, pencil, ruler	More able students to generate more accurate vision of planned wood joint	Spatial awareness and mental vision of planned wood joint
30 mins Practical activity	Tutor to guide students on marking out their mortice and tenon joint	Students to mark out accurately their mortice and tenon joint	Class set of timber, set square, marking gauge, pencil, ruler	More able students to generate more accurate wood joint	Students to think about demonstration and repeat process for themselves – special awareness
10 mins Self and peer assessment	Tutor to monitor and evaluate completed wood joints	Students to mark and evaluate their wood joint and those of their peers	Assessment sheets	Embedding knowledge for all students from feedback given by Tutor and peer assessment	English skills – students to evaluate and review their work in a written report
5 mins Plenary	Review of learning objectives	Q&A session to reflect on learning	Why the mortice and tenon joint is used and how it is marked out		Reflective students – consider what they have learnt to secure learning

Level 2 Diploma in Construction and the Built Environment

Lesson plan 3 (craft area option 3)

Unit 5 Create the built environment: Using tools – Painting and Decorating

Centre name:

Tutor/lecturer(s):

Aims & objectives

- To consider surface preparation for painting

SB = Student Book
ADR = Assessment and Delivery Resource

Learning objectives

- All students should understand what surface preparation is
- Most should be able to identify the correct tools and equipment to successfully prepare a surface for ready for painting

Timings reflect one typical session within the GLH block of 3 hours allocated in the SOW

Total lesson time: 90 minutes

Timing/ Content	Tutor activity	Learner activity	Resources	Individualised activity/differentiation	Personal Learning and Thinking Skills	Functional Skills
5 mins Welcome learners and register	Check health and safety of the room Take a register	Enter room in accordance with normal procedures and settle quickly	Register			
10 mins Starter	Tutor to give introduction to the importance of surface preparation	Pupils to listen and take notes on tutors explanation	SB p152	Discussion with Q and A session on surface preparation and why it is needed	Effective participators – engage in debate and encourage development of ideas	English skills through debate and language skills

Time/Activity	Tutor activity	Pupil activity	Resources	Differentiation	
10 mins	Tutor to explain the correct way in which to prepare the surface ready for painting	Write down clear notes that explain how the surface is best prepared	Whiteboard and projector ADR p175	Direction for weaker pupils to clearly draw and annotate the best practice for preparing surfaces	IT skills – more able pupils encouraged to prepare short presentation
25 mins Alternative ways of preparing surfaces	Tutor to demonstrate to pupils different ways to prepare surfaces	Pupils to watch demonstration and to clearly visualise how to prepare surfaces	Range of surfaces in different conditions – dust, dirt, grease and old paint finishes that are cracked or flaking	More able pupils to generate more accurate vision of how surfaces are best prepared	Spatial awareness and mental vision of different preparation methods
25 mins Practical activity	Tutor to guide pupils on preparing surfaces	Pupils to carry out a range of different surface preparations	Class set of alternative surface finishes	More able pupils to generate more accurate and quality surface preparations	Pupils to think about demonstration and repeat process for themselves – special awareness
10 mins Self and peer assessment	Tutor to monitor and evaluate completed surface preparations	Pupils to mark and evaluate their surface preparations	Assessment sheets	Embedding knowledge for all pupils from feedback given by tutor and peer assessment	
5 mins Plenary	Review of learning objectives	Q&A session to reflect on learning	Why the surface is prepared before painting takes place		Reflective learners – consider what they have learnt to secure learning

Level 2 Diploma in Construction and the Built Environment

Lesson plan 4 (craft area option 4)

Unit 5: Create the built environment: Using Tools – Building services

Centre name:

Tutor/lecturer(s):

Aims & objectives

- Learn to demonstrate the safe and correct use of the tools appropriate to the task
- Maintain a tidy working area
- Handle tools with appropriate care and clean after use

SB = Student Book

ADR = Assessment and Delivery Resource

Total lesson time: 120 minutes

Learning objectives

- Know about health and safety procedures in a construction craft environment
- Understand the safe working characteristics and safe use of materials
- Be able to use tools safely and effectively to produce a practical outcome

Timings reflect one typical session within the GLH block of 3 hours allocated in the SOW

Timing/ Content	Teacher activity	Student activity	Resources	Individualised activity/differentiation	Personal learning and thinking skills	Functional skills
5 mins Welcome students and register	Check health and safety of the room Take a register	Enter room in accordance with normal procedures and settle quickly	Register			
5 mins Starter	Introduce starter: SB How many joints?	Students work in pairs to think about how many joints may be in the plumbing system of a house.	SB page 164	Record estimate on paper and feed back to class	Effective participators – able to discuss ideas and communicate Team workers – able to manage and encourage input from others in group	

Time / Topic	Teacher activity	Student activity	Resources	Differentiation / support	PLTS / skills
10 mins Identification of materials	Remind students what the practical element of the project involves Show the selection of materials they will get during the lesson	Students identify the materials they will use during lesson	One piece of copper pipe per student (enough to mark out and cut 3 equal pieces to join) One compression tee per student ADR p176	Identification and communication of materials	
10 mins Identification of tools	Allow student's time in which to try and identify the tools required to mark out, cut and join three lengths of copper pipe.	Students to name the tools needed to complete the task	Range of tools for students to see and select from. Need: pencil, steel rule, tape measure, hacksaw, adjustable spanner, bench hook, file	Identification and selection of appropriate tools for the task.	Effective participators – can discuss issues with others they may not know so well
25 mins Demo and first part of practical task	Demonstration of marking out and cutting copper pipe	Students to watch demonstration then prepare the 3 lengths of copper pipe by marking out, cutting and removing burr.	Copper pipe and appropriate tools carry out the task	One to one demos for students who need extra support.	
25 mins	Demonstration of jointing methods using a compression tee	Students to watch demonstration then join 3 lengths of copper pipe using the compression tee	Copper pipe, compression tee, adjustable spanner	One to one demos for students who need extra support.	
35 mins	Take photographs and print out as students finish the practical task Record of activity	Students are to stick image of their work onto sheet and then record in a flow chart format how the process they completed	ADR activity p165–6	Embedding knowledge for all students	Math skills – students calculate angles correctly
5 mins Plenary	Review of learning outcomes	Q&A session to reflect on learning	What are the important stages to remember? What tools are needed? What materials are needed?	Embedding knowledge for all students	Reflective students – consider what they have learnt to secure learning

5.1   Job roles and responsibilities: The construction team

Student Book
pp 112–113

1 In the table below, tick the box if you think that the correct job title is with its correct description; if you think it is incorrect, write the correct description on the line in the table.

2 Complete the middle column of the table, to classify the job titles as craft, professional, supervisory, technical, management, technician or operative.

Job title	Classification	Description
Trade foreman _____		Is the supervising officer during the construction phase. Is in overall charge of ensuring that the building is constructed to the required standards. Also deals with contract administration such as issuing instructions, extensions of time and certificates to authorise payment.
Quantity surveyor (QS) _____		Agrees monthly valuations and the final account with the equivalent person working for the client. Will also produce budgets and forecasts of costs, and may be involved in the measurement and payment of subcontractors.
Ganger _____		Leads the management team on large projects. Is accountable for the completion of the project, on time, within budget and to quality standards.
Architect _____		Sometimes known as a site agent. Manages the site and act as the contractor's representative.
Joiner _____		Organises and supervises operatives and craftspeople. On small projects, is in overall control.
Planner _____		Organises and supervises craft area, and may provide technical support, quality control and advice specific to the craft.
General foreman _____		Supervises a group of non-craft operatives such as drain-layers, concreters and ground-workers.
Plumber _____		Produces contract programmes, often in the form of Gantt charts. Plans site activities to ensure that the project is completed on time.
Buyer _____		Schedules materials, obtains quotations and places orders for materials to arrive on site to meet the planner's programme of works.
Building services engineer _____		Assists the site manager in establishing levels, setting out the works on site, ensuring that drains are to the correct falls. Carries out quality control checks to ensure that work is within specified tolerances.

Job title	Classification	Description
Electrician _____		Acts as the architect's on-site representative to ensure that the construction on site is to the architect's design and specification.
Painter and decorator _____		Works in a joinery workshop manufacturing items made out of wood for installation on site, such as windows, door frames and staircases.
Carpenter _____		Is the onsite woodworker constructing formwork, floors, roofs, internal partitions, and fixing joinery items.
Bricklayer _____		Lays bricks and blocks, and installs other components associated with brickwork such as DPCs, lintels, cavity wall insulation and wall ties.
Project manager _____		Installs electrical services, power distribution circuits, lighting services, control systems and alarms to buildings.
Site manager _____		Installs sanitary goods, hot and cold water systems, soil, vent and waste pipework, gas services and domestic heating systems.
Construction operative _____		Installs more complex mechanical and electrical heating and air-conditioning systems to larger non-domestic construction.
Site engineer _____		Provides the final decorative coatings – usually painting and wallpaper hanging.
Clerk of works _____		A general site worker – may include: drain-layer, forklift driver, concreter or general labourer.
Safety officer _____		Deals with all aspects of health and safety, including inductions, training, safety briefings and inspections.

5.2   Health and safety legislation

**Student Book
pp 114–115**

1   Complete the mind map below using 'health and safety legislation' as the key word. Think of as many 'branches' as you can.

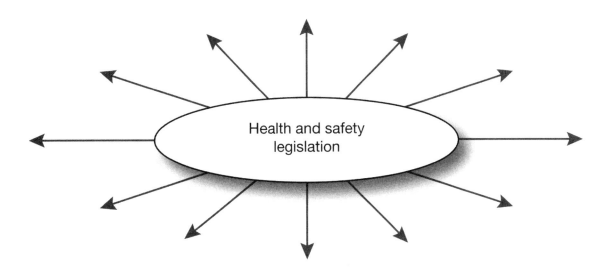

2   Imagine you are a health and safety inspector, and you are visiting your classroom. Go and look around the class and create a risk assessment chart of all the tools, equipment and machines. Describe any possible risks that could occur and make notes on how the tools, equipment and machines should be maintained. Also look for hazards such as storage or dust extraction problems. Create a chart to show what you have found.

5.3   Personal protective equipment (PPE)

Student Book
pp 116–117

1   Look the picture below. What types of PPE are shown here? Write your answers alongside the picture.

2   There are nine items of PPE hidden in this wordsearch. Use the clues to find them all.

H	A	R	D	H	A	T	S	H	G	H	M	L	W
F	I	D	F	B	N	S	H	I	G	N	G	T	E
B	S	G	D	G	J	I	I	U	U	L	K	J	A
A	S	A	F	E	T	Y	G	L	O	V	E	S	R
R	A	A	R	T	M	K	S	A	M	T	S	U	D
R	F	H	F	A	S	K	T	S	A	G	E	T	E
I	S	H	E	E	Q	G	X	Z	Z	Y	K	M	F
E	S	M	T	Y	T	V	W	X	Y	S	A	H	E
R	A	S	A	R	E	Y	A	F	E	R	F	H	N
C	S	F	E	T	M	N	B	M	G	L	R	A	D
R	A	S	R	R	W	A	N	O	D	L	C	I	E
E	F	T	D	U	T	S	M	A	O	R	Y	W	R
A	E	Y	R	E	S	P	I	R	A	T	O	R	S
M	P	H	I	G	H	V	I	S	V	E	S	T	S
O	S	E	S	S	A	L	G	Y	T	E	F	A	S

Clues!

1. To protect your head from falling debris
2. Usually steel toe-capped to protect feet from heavy objects
3. To protect your eyes from flying debris
4. So that your hands won't be damaged by abrasive materials or chemicals
5. So that your ears are protected from excessive noise on site
6. To offer your hands some protection from chemicals
7. Worn to protect you from breathing in dust
8. Wear this so you can be easily seen
9. You use it when fumes are toxic

5.4   Access equipment

Student Book
pp 118–119

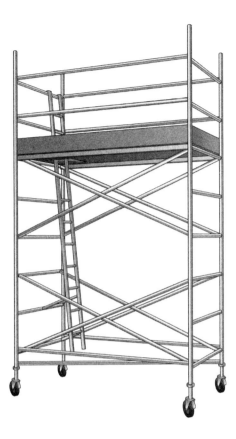

Study the image and answer the following questions.

1   What is the name for the type of scaffold shown?

2   This type of scaffold is usually made of either steel or what other material?

3   How would you determine the maximum safe height when using this type of scaffold?

4   What must be done with the wheels before using the scaffold, and why?

5.5A   Brickwork 1: Bricks and blocks

Student Book
pp 120–121

1   Label the parts of this brick

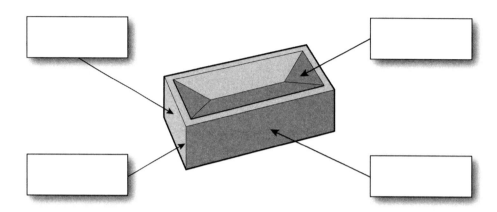

2   Design a freestanding wall in the space below choosing your own amount of bricks. When you have finished, work out the overall height and length.

Height =   Length =   Number of bricks used =

5.5B　Brickwork 1: Bricks and blocks

**Student Book
pp 120–121**

1　Label the dimensions of this brick with the correct sizes.

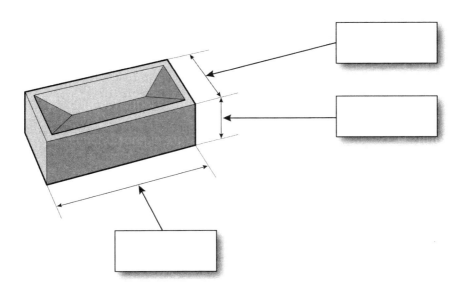

2　Look for images and diagrams of special types or bricks. Sketch and label two or three examples below.

　　　　141

5.6   Brickwork 2: Sundry materials

Student Book
pp 122–123

1   Complete the following paragraph.

In any building, a damp- _____ course, is required by _____ and is put in place to keep out moisture. You will have seen in the news the damage that can be done to houses by floodwater, but the damage that _____ can cause can be just as bad. The _____ - _____ _____ stops the _____ from rain that soaks into the ground or groundwater itself from getting into the structure of the building.

A damp-proof course is a layer of moisture-resistant material, the same width as the brickwork or blockwork wall, positioned at 150 mm _____ ground level. There are various _____ used for DPCs including PVC, polythene, Class B Engineers, _____ or slate.

moisture   bitumen   proof   damp   above   law   materials   damp   proof   course

2   After reading the topic materials in the student book, create a mind map of the information you have learnt. You can use the one below as a starting point to help if you need to.

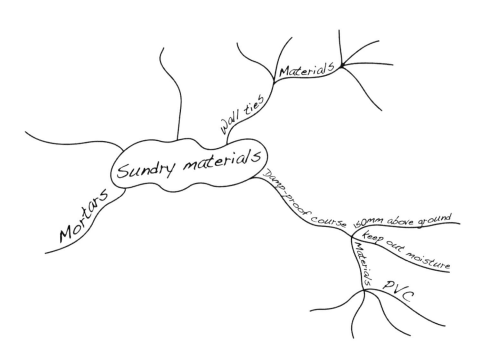

5.7   Brickwork 3: Tools

Student Book
pp 124–125

1   Look at the tools that your teacher has put out on a workbench in the classroom.

- brick trowel
- pointing trowel
- steel float
- wood float
- hand hawk
- joint raker (chariot)
- jointer
- tape measure
- brick hammer
- club or lump hammer
- claw hammer

- scutch or comb hammer
- bolster chisel
- cold chisel
- plugging chisel
- scutch comb chisel
- spirit level
- boat level
- line and pins
- corner block
- tingle plate

Try to identify as many tools as possible. Draw them and give each its correct name.

2   Imagine you are a bricklayer. You have been asked to suggest ideas for a wall at the front of a homeowner's garden. You should research and investigate what different types of walls and decorative finishes are available. Write down your findings.

3   Continuing the scenario above, work in pairs, one playing the bricklayer, the other the homeowner. The bricklayer must try to sell a type of wall to the homeowner. Describe in detail the type of walls available, what the benefits are of each and how they will be built. See which wall wins!

143

5.8   Brickwork 4: Bonding

Student Book
pp 126–127

1   Describe the three main types of brickwork bonds. Explain the differences between them in the table below.

Brickwork bond	Description	Differences to other bonds

2   Take a tour of your school with paper and clipboard in hand. Draw a range of different types of brickwork bonds that you can see. For each type, explain how the bonding helps spread the load of the structure.

5.9 Brickwork 5: Laying bricks to line

Student Book
pp 128–129

1 In pairs, produce a step-by-step guide, using Powerpoint, to laying bricks in a straight line. Take time to work out the clearest, easiest-to-follow instructions, and show each clearly. When you have finished, give a presentation to the rest of the class to show good practice for this process.

2 Imagine you are a brick manufacturer. Investigate the best way in which bricks can be made, how this is done and what tools, equipment and machines are involved. Write notes on all aspects of what you discover.

3 To extend the activity above, think of the health and safety hazards that are involved in brick manufacture, and then do some research into how this might affect how much you might sell your products for.

5.10   Brickwork 6: Jointing and quality control

**Student Book
pp 130–131**

1   Imagine you are a bricklaying foreman or site manager. Pretend that you are going around the construction site. Name the quality control checks that you will be carrying out and explain how you would go about remedying any problems that might have occurred. Write down the tour, the checks you have carried out and what is to be done to make up for any poor quality work.

2   Fill in the information missing from the table.

	Comment	Pass/Fail
Brick selection and blend	Bricks exhibited slight variations in colour and size and carbon deposits / firing burn marks were present on some bricks, but most packs had similar qualities. I have blended them in the finished wall to provide an aesthetically pleasing outcome.	**Pass**
	The mortar was mixed by the technician at the central batching plant. I reworked the mortar at the spot board so that the mortar could be rolled and spread with good workability and consistency.	**Pass**
Pointing and jointing	I used a jointer to produce a bucket-handle joint and this was completed in the correct order: perps first, followed by the bed joint.	**Pass**
Correct brick orientation		**Pass**
General cleanliness	Some drying out still required at time of taking photograph, but brickwork is generally clean and well presented. There are no smears or splashes of mortar present on the face of the brickwork.	
Vertical joint line	Joints on alternate courses in line when checked with edge of spirit level.	
	Well presented attractive brickwork.	**Pass**
Dimensional tolerance		**Pass**

3   Fill in the information missing from this table.

Joint	Name	Description
profile		The most common brickwork joint and the quickest and easiest to complete using a jointing iron. Sheds water easily, so suitable for outdoor work
profile	Recessed joint	
profile	Flush joint	
profile		Produced using a pointing trowel. Joint slopes slightly, allowing water to run off the surface of the joint and down the face of the brick easily. Suitable for exposed conditions.

5.11 Carpentry and Joinery 1: Hand tools and equipment

Student Book
pp 132–133

1 Look at the photos below – can you name the tools shown here?

2 Pretend you are a carpenter or joiner and you are about to cut a sheet of plywood using a portable circular saw. On a separate sheet of paper describe, with the aid of sketches, all the safety procedures you will have to carry out from start to finish to ensure you cut the plywood safely.

3 Complete a mind map for one of the three following key words – how many words and issues can you think of that link to that word.

- portable power tools

- hand tools

- health and safety on site

5.12   Carpentry and Joinery 2: Softwoods and hardwoods

**Student Book
pp 134–135**

1   Fill in the missing information.

Type of softwood/hardwood	Appearance and use	Coniferous or deciduous
Cedar, western red		
Fir, douglas		
Parana pine		
Yew		
Ash		
Beech		
Mahogany		
Oak		
Walnut		

2 Describe five differences between softwoods and hardwoods, using the table below.

Softwoods	Hardwoods

5.13 Carpentry and Joinery 3: Manufactured boards

Student Book pp 136–137

1 Fill in the missing details in the table below.

Type of manufactured board	Suitable for exterior work	Easy for planing/cutting	Weight: light/medium/heavy	Description
Plywood	Yes		Medium	
		Intermediate	Heavy	The inner part is made from strips of softwood glued together. The core is then sandwiched between two layers of wood. Thickness is usually 12 to 25 mm.
Chipboard	No		Heavy	
MDF			Heavy	
	No		Light	Usually available in sheets that are 3–6 mm in thickness. Often used for covering floors, doors and drawer bottoms. Also has a smooth finish and can be easily decorated.

2 Complete the table below to show your knowledge of what manufactured boards would or could be used when constructing a specific room of a house.

Room	Type of manufactured board	Uses for the room
Bedroom		
Kitchen		
Bathroom		
Loft/loft conversion		
Dining room		
Stairs		
Conservatory		
Hallway		

5.14   Carpentry and Joinery 4: Miscellaneous materials

Student Book
pp 138–139

1   In pairs, research which of these combinations work successfully, and which fail.

Adhesive to be used	Materials to be glued	Success or failure
PVA	Pine to pine	
Liquid tensol cement	Oak to oak	
Araldite	Polystyrene to polystyrene	
PVA	Pine to pine	
Cascamite	Oak to acrylic	
PVA	Pine to polystyrene	
Liquid tensol cement	Acrylic to acrylic	
Araldite	Pine to pine	
Cascamite	Polystyrene to pine	

2   Go round your classroom and try to identify as many miscellaneous materials as you can. Draw out a table as shown, filling in the missing details.

Name of miscellaneous material	What it is used for	Advantages of using the material

5.15   Carpentry and Joinery 5: Quality control

Student Book
pp 140–141

1   Look at the table below and fill in the missing information about timber defects.

Description	Seasoning or natural defect	Name of defect
Caused mainly by disease, this is shrinkage of the inner trunk whilst the outer stays its original shape.		
Marks the start of branch growth, can be 'dead' which are often loose and fall out.		
Caused through shrinkage during drying; most common in flat sawn boards.		
Cracks around outside of the log, caused by the inside staying its original size whilst the outer shrinks.		
Caused by either poor stacking or seasoning, the wood is almost ruined and can only be used as short lengths.		

2   Take an A3 piece of paper and fold it into quarters. In each section, draw and describe one of these four conversion methods:

■ through and through

■ tangential

■ quarter

■ boxed heart

5.16   Carpentry and Joinery 6: Efficient use of resources

Student Book
pp 142–143

1   Design a storage unit for sheet glass to allow it to be retrieved easily, but also to prevent any scratches or breakage during storage. Think about how you might keep the sheets separated, and by what distance. What would you do if you wanted to make the storage unit portable or lightweight? Consider the materials you use carefully.

2   In the table below, describe how you would best transport and store the materials named.

Material	Best form of transportation	Best form of storage
Roof tiles		
Bricks		
Sheet material, e.g. plywood		
Pine		

3   Work in pairs. One of you is to play a disgruntled customer who has just received a delivery of defaced goods (for example, most of a sheet glass order has been scratched); the other of you is to play the supplier. The 'customer' must imagine what you would say in a phone call to the supplier; the 'supplier' has to think how best to handle the angry customer.

Write down the phone conversation and decide on the final outcome of the call.

5.17 Carpentry and Joinery 7: Wood joints

Student Book
pp 144–145

1   Your task is to successfully construct by hand a joint from the choice of three available.

Afterwards, write an account on how you felt it went, whether it was hard or easy, time-consuming or done in no time. Finally, comment on the quality – give yourself a mark out of ten.

Through mortise and tenon

Lap joint

Mited butt joint

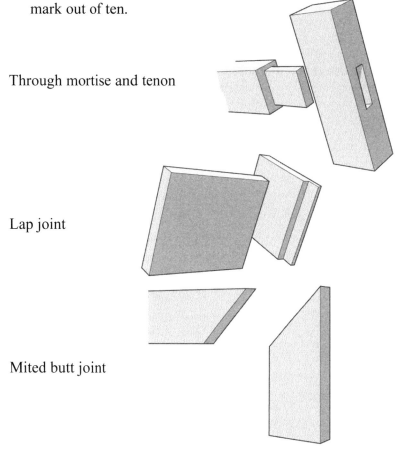

2   Cut a piece each of MDF, pine and hardwood such as oak in half. Explain the differences when cutting these three woods.

_____

_____

_____

_____

_____

_____

3   In groups of three, apply a selection of finishes to a piece of pine. Produce a table like the one below and fill in your comments as a group.

Type of wood	Finish applied	Comment regarding appearance

5.18   Painting and decorating 1: Decoration

Student Book
pp 146–147

1   Choose a room in your own home, preferably a bedroom or lounge, and present a proposal for its redecoration. Your proposal should include the following points:

- Colour schemes – walls, ceiling, woodwork, soft furnishings etc.

- Use of texture – e.g. paint, wallpaper, textured coatings, soft furnishings etc.

- Durability – e.g. resistance of finishes to scuffing etc if in a busy area

- Use of light.

- Furniture.

2   Draw a plan of your room and identify how the furniture will be arranged once the decoration has been completed.

5.19   Painting and decorating 2: Tools and equipment

Student Book
 pp 148–149

1   Complete the table below to identify the tools and equipment required to carry out a decorating job.

Surface	Specification	Tools and equipment required
Ceiling	Remove existing Anaglypta, make good, apply 800 grade lining paper and apply two coats of vinyl matt emulsion in white	
Walls	Prepare previously emulsion-painted walls, make good, cross line with 800 grade lining paper and hang vinyl wallpaper as supplied by customer	
Windows	uPVC – no treatment required	
Doors, architraves and skirtings	Prepare previously gloss painted surfaces and apply two coats of undercoat and one coat of gloss finish in white	

2   Use your knowledge of painting and decorating tools and equipment to label the diagram with the names and uses of the items shown.

5.20   Painting and decorating 3: Materials

**Student Book
pp 150–151**

1 You are decorating the lounge in a newly built house. Complete the table to identify the materials required to complete the work

Surface	Specification	Materials required
Ceiling	Textured stipple finish	
Walls	Matt finish in magnolia	
Hardwood dado rail and doors	Mahogany-coloured satin finish	
Skirtings and architraves	Knot, prime and stop and provide eggshell finish in white	
Hardwood floor	Clear satin finish	

2 Assuming that the room is 2.3 metres high, 5.7 metres long and 3.9 metres wide, calculate the amount of magnolia emulsion paint required to apply three coats to the walls, and the amount of white emulsion paint required to apply two coats to the ceiling. The spreading rate for emulsion paint is approximately 13 m^2 per litre.

5.21 Painting and decorating 4: Painting

Student Book
pp 152–153

1   In the table below, complete the last column by indicating whether the material can be used internally, externally or both.

Surface coating	Oil- or water-based?	Description	Internal/external use
Acrylic primer/undercoat		Developed to perform the functions of both primer and undercoat – can be used on a wide range of surfaces but not on bare metal	
Alkali-resisting primer		Primer that is used on surfaces that are alkaline in nature to prevent the alkali from attacking subsequent paint films	
Zinc phosphate		A rust-inhibiting metal primer developed to replace old lead-based primers	
Emulsion		Available in matt, silk and semi-sheen finishes and used extensively on walls and ceilings	
Eggshell		A decorative semi-sheen finish – not as hardwearing as gloss finish	
Bituminous paint		Bitumen-based finish used to protect iron and steelwork, storage tanks, cast-iron gutters and concrete	

2   Complete the second column in the table by indicating whether the coating is oil – or water-based.

5.22   Painting and decorating 5: Wallpapering

**Student Book
pp 154–155**

The diagram below shows the plan of a room that is to be wallpapered.

1   Calculate the number of rolls of lining paper required to line the ceiling ready for painting.

2   Calculate the number of rolls of vinyl wallpaper required to paper the walls. The paper has a straight pattern match that repeats every 50 cm.

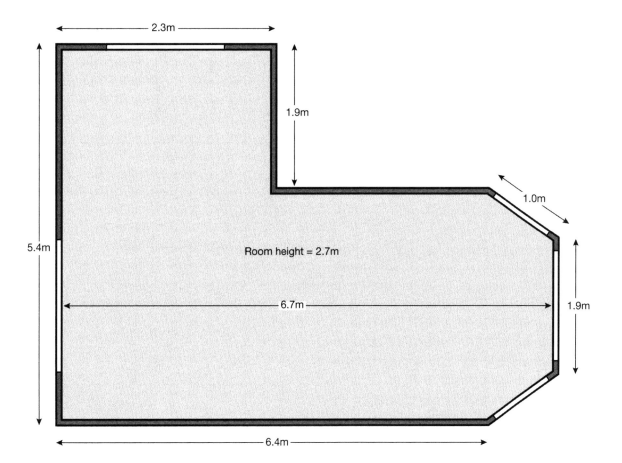

5.23   Painting and decorating 6: Quality control and common defects

Student Book
pp 156–157

1   The table below shows a number of common defects found in surface coatings. Complete the table by providing an explanation of how the defect could be prevented.

Defect	Appearance	Prevention
Bittiness	Paint finish feels gritty or appears dirty	
Discolouration	Surface finish fades or becomes paler in colour	
Fat edges	Thick ridges of paint along edges of a painted surface	
Grinning	The previous colour can be seen through a finishing coat	
Orange peel	Surface has a slight texture to the finish like the peel of an orange	
Saponification	Paint film becomes soft or sticky. Sometimes a brown soapy liquid appears on the surface	

2   Working in pairs, imagine you are responsible for quality control on a decorating project. On your project inspection, you have listed a number of defects in the wallpapering.

- Loss of embossing
- Creasing
- Paste staining
- Peeling
- Ragged edges

Together, produce a brief report on the most probable cause of each of these defects, and explain what how each could be corrected.

5.24A Building services 1: Tools and equipment (electrical)

**Student Book
pp 158–159**

1   Fill up the toolbox with typical tools used by an electrician. Use either images from catalogues, magazines or the internet, or your own sketches.

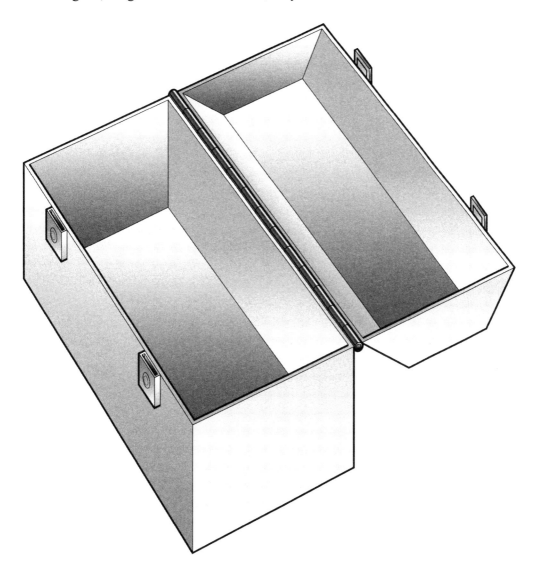

2   List the tools you have chosen below and explain what they are used for.

_____

_____

_____

_____

_____

_____

5.24B   Building services 1: Tools and equipment (plumbing)

**Student Book
pp 158–159**

1   Fill up the toolbox with typical tools used by a plumber. Use either images from catalogues, magazines or the internet, or your own sketches.

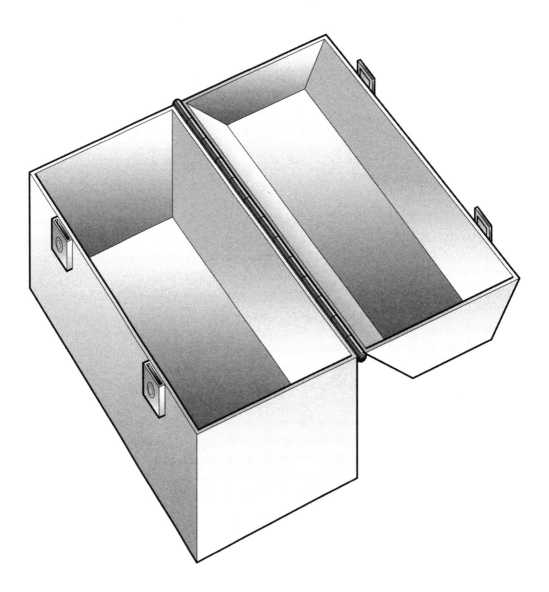

2   List the tools you have chosen below and explain what they are used for.

_____

_____

_____

_____

_____

_____

166

5.25   Building services 2: Materials (plumbing)

1   Find definitions for the different properties of materials.

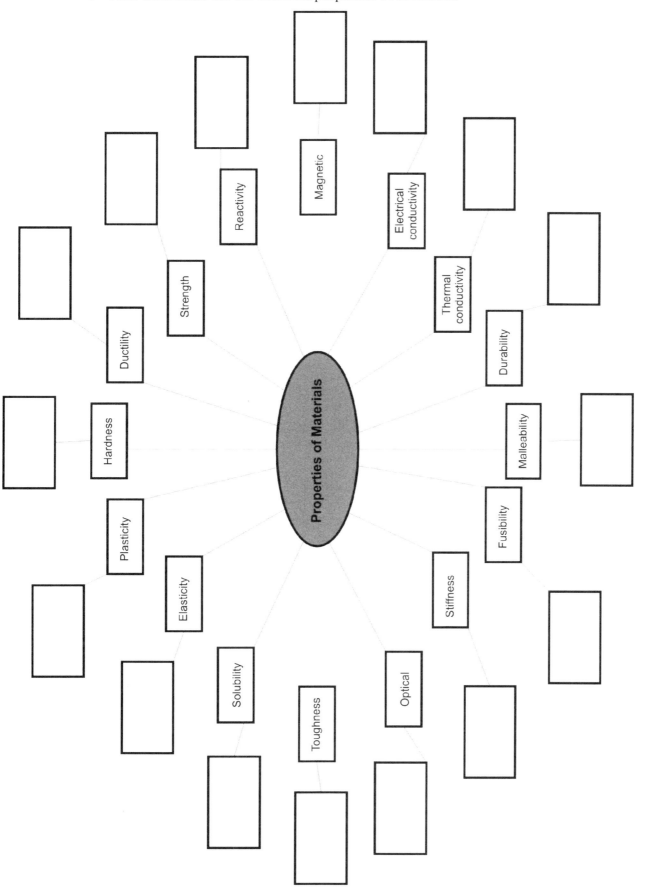

5.26   Building services 3: Materials (electrical)

**Student Book
pp 162–163**

1. Look at the following diagram of cable types. Fill in the missing information, including a coloured diagram of the type of cable on the third row of the diagram.

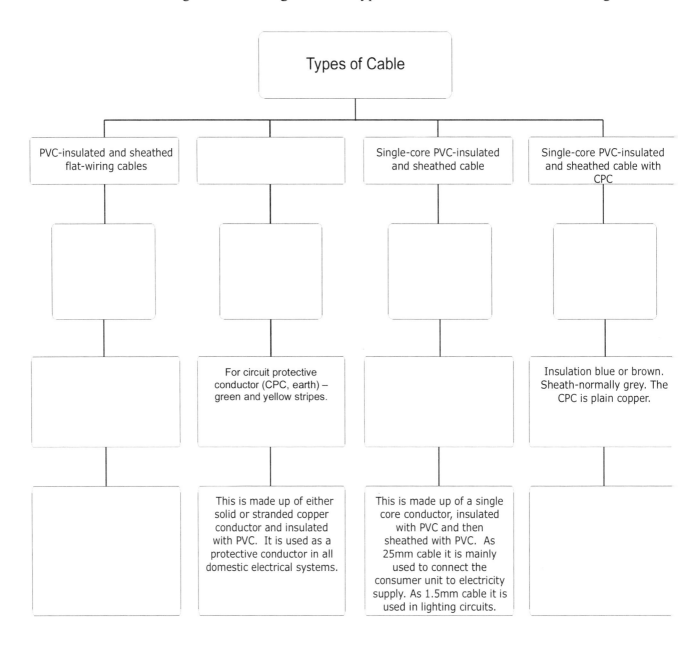

Types of Cable

| PVC-insulated and sheathed flat-wiring cables | | Single-core PVC-insulated and sheathed cable | Single-core PVC-insulated and sheathed cable with CPC |

| | For circuit protective conductor (CPC, earth) – green and yellow stripes. | | Insulation blue or brown. Sheath-normally grey. The CPC is plain copper. |

| | This is made up of either solid or stranded copper conductor and insulated with PVC. It is used as a protective conductor in all domestic electrical systems. | This is made up of a single core conductor, insulated with PVC and then sheathed with PVC. As 25mm cable it is mainly used to connect the consumer unit to electricity supply. As 1.5mm cable it is used in lighting circuits. | |

5.27   Building services 4: Jointing methods

1   Carry out some research on the following types of compression fittings. Find an image and cut out or sketch each, then describe where it would be used.

Name of fitting	Image	Description
Straight adaptors		
Straight couplers		
Tap connectors		
Stop ends		
Tees		
Elbows		
Wall-plate elbows		
Bent tank connectors		
Straight tank connectors		

2   Using the following provided materials construct the following design:

- ■ 2 x 90-degree 15mm elbows

- ■ 1 x straight tank connectors

- ■ 1 x 15mm tee

- ■ 1 x 1m 15mm pipe

- ■ 1 x 15mm compression 90-degree elbow

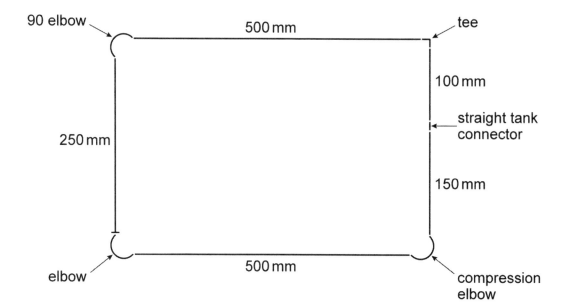

5.28   Building services 5: Quality control and defects

**Student Book
pp 166–167**

1   Write a definition for the following terms.

Term	Definition
Quality control	
Aesthetically pleasing	
Blockage	
Non-live test	
Live test	
Termination	

2   In your project work, you will have to carry out a practical activity. As part of this, you will have to carry out quality control procedures. List them on this flow chart.

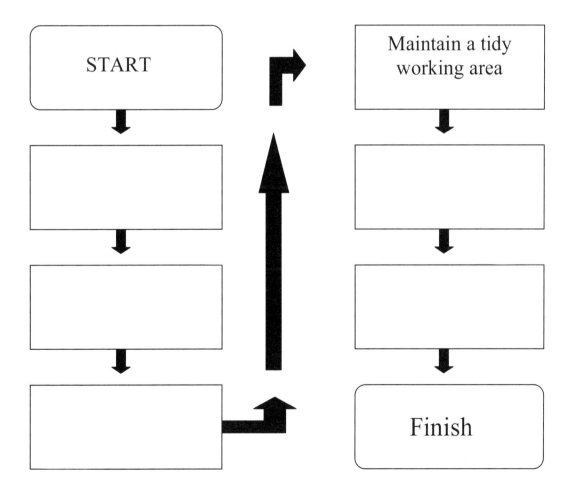

5.29   Brickwork: Practical activity

**Student Book
pp 120–131**

1   Follow these steps to roll mortar.

- ■ **Step 1:** Collect equipment needed for practical activity.

- ■ **Step 2:** Collect mortar

- ■ **Step 3:** Wet sport board using water and a bucket and brush.

- ■ **Step 4:** Scoop an appropriate amount of mortar away from the pile.

- ■ **Step 5:** Begin rolling mortar by scooping it up with the brick trowel using a twisting action.

- ■ **Step 6:** Continue to roll mortar until it has a smooth and workable appearance.

- ■ **Step 7:** Place mortar onto spot board ready to use.

Resources you will need include:

- ■ Bucket and brush
- ■ Water
- ■ Mortar (sand and lime mix)
- ■ Shovel
- ■ Brick trowel
- ■ Spot board

- ■ Stand
- ■ Hard hat
- ■ Protective clothing
- ■ Gloves
- ■ Boots
- ■ High visibility vest

Health and safety tips

Ensure correct PPE is worn.
Wear gloves or barrier cream to prevent reactions to mortar.
Avoid contact of mortar with eyes and skin.

---

2   Answer the following questions:

- ■ Why is lime added to the mortar mix?

- ■ What are the most common mortar mixes?

- ■ Why is a sand and lime mix used for your project?

5.30   Carpentry and joinery: Practical activity

Student Book
pp 132–145

1   Follow these steps to mark out a mortice joint.

■ **Step 1:** Complete visual check on wood to ensure there are no defects, e.g. knocks, warping etc.

■ **Step 2:** Check the wood plain (jack plain or smooth plain) to ensure it is set correctly.

■ **Step 3:** Mark the wood using a tri square.

■ **Step 4:** Clamp the wood into position.

■ **Step 5:** Plain one side of the wood to ensure it is both straight and smooth. Be careful if dealing with end grain.

■ **Step 6:** Check the wood is square with a tri square. If not, repeat the steps 3, 4 and 5.

■ **Step 7:** Set up the mortise gauge to correct dimensions/position.

■ **Step 8:** Mark out mortise joint with mortise gauge, pencil, sheet rule and tri square.

■ **Step 9:** Check process has been done correctly and accurately. If not repeat from step 3.

Resources you will need include:

■ Timber

■ Pencil

■ Tri square

■ Jack plain or smoothing plain

■ Sheet rules

■ Mortise gauge

■ G clamp

Health and safety tips

Make sure the plain is set correctly plain with the direction of the grain.
If plaining end grain a piece of scrap wood should be used to avoid slipping or plain into the centre from both sides.

---

2   Complete the table below, naming as many tools and equipment associated with marking out a mortice and tenon joint as you can and explaining what they are used for.

Name of tool or equipment	What it is used for

5.31   Painting and decorating: Practical activity

Student Book
pp 146–157

1   Follow these steps to prepare a surface for painting and decorating:

- Step 1 Identify the defects that appear on the wood, e.g. cracks, previous paint etc

- Step 2 Clean all surfaces to ensure that they are smooth, free from dust or grease

- Step 3 Choose the method most appropriate to apply to the timber from the following:

Sugar soap	Cleaning material – looks a bit like sugar when in powder form; mix with water to use
Liquid paint remover	Solvent- or water-based – it is painted onto old paint films so they blister and can be scrapped off.
Shellac knotting	Methylated spirit-based – applied over knots in timber to stop resin seeping out and damaging paint film.
Fillers and stoppers	Powder-based or ready-mixed – used to fill cracks, holes or other surface defects before paining.

- Step 4 Apply treatment to timber to create suitable quality finish

- Step 5 Check all processes have been done correctly to ensure that surface is prepared thoroughly. If this is incorrect repeat from step 1. Be sure to wear goggles/aprons/gloves etc.

Resources you will need include:

- A range of pre treated timber, e.g. already painted/cracks etc

- Gloves

- Goggles

- Apron

- Four treatments (See table)

- Paint scrapper

- Wire wool

175

5.32 Building services: Practical activity

Student Book
pp 146–157

1   Follow these steps to prepare a surface for marking out and cutting pipe and creating a plumbing joint with a compression tee.

- **Step 1:** Collect materials needed for activity.

- **Step 2:** Mark out three lengths of copper pipe using a tape measure/steel rule and pencil. You will need three lengths of 150mm.

- **Step 3:** Cut the copper pipe using a bench hook and hacksaw.

- **Step 4:** Remove the burr from the pipe by filing.

- **Step 5:** Remove the nut and olive from one part of the compression tee.

- **Step 6:** Thread one length of copper pipe through the nut then the olive.

- **Step 7:** Insert the pipe into the compression tee.

- **Step 8:** Slide the olive and nut down to the fitting and hand tighten.

- **Step 9:** Tighten the nut using an adjustable spanner.

- **Step 10:** Repeat step 5 to 9 with the other two parts of the compression tee.

Resources you will need include:

- Copper pipe
- Compression Tee
- Steel Rule
- Tape measure
- Pencil
- Hacksaw
- Bench hook
- File
- Adjustable spanner

Health and safety tips

Ensure correct use of equipment.
Watch out for sharp edges and burr on edge of copper pipe.
Ensure adjustable spanner is adjusted to size to prevent slipping.

6

Value and Use of the Built Environment: Communities

nit overview

In this unit the sustainability of a community is investigated. This is studied from the perspective of social and community issues, focusing on the economic impact of buildings and their life cycle issues. The use of sustainable practices and materials are examined by the student, involving local sourcing, site practices and sustainable maintenance of the built environment. The needs of our future generations and the scarcity of resources, needs to be factored into the design and any current building program.

The contribution that the built environment makes to societies and the wider community is examined in the second learning objective. Here the student investigates the role of both private and public housing and how each has contributed to the well being of the community. The type of accommodation, the market place and the issues for first time buyers are all current issues. The local property economy is examined in terms of house prices and the factors that affect these.

The built environment has several areas that need improvement and these are examined in the third learning outcome. Here the issues of safety and security are evaluated. Good clean safe and secure accommodation and work environment has a great benefit to our built environment and the communities living within it. This is an issue as our population demographics get older.

The final outcome looks and examines the job roles in the use of the built environment. These involve not only the craft and operative levels but also the supervisory and managerial levels maintaining the built environment. Hence the professional roles of the building surveyor, estate agent, maintenance engineer and facilities manager and their professional organisations are examined in detail, with regard to qualifications, training and progression routes.

Links with other units

Level 1
- Unit 5: Value and use of the built environment
- Unit 6: Maintenance of the built environment

Level 2
- Unit 7: Value and use of the built environment: Facilities management

Level 3
- Unit 6: Value and use of the built environment: Adding value to the wider community
- Unit 7: Value and use of the built environment: Protecting and maintaining

Topics covered	Edexcel unit learning outcomes
Sustainability	Know how sustainability affects the built environment
Impact upon the community	Be able to evaluate the contribution of the built environment to society and communities
Improving the built environment	Understand how the built environment can be improved to benefit individuals and communities
Job roles and responsibilities	Understand the job roles, progression routes, occupational structures and the importance of teamwork relating to building maintenance and facilities management

How this unit will be assessed

Assessment is based on the student being able to demonstrate that they have met four learning outcomes. These are:

LO 6.1 Know how sustainability affects the built environment

LO 6.2 Be able to evaluate the contribution of the built environment to society and communities

LO 6.3 Understand how the built environment can be improved to benefit individuals and communities

LO 6.4 Understand the job roles, progression routes, occupational structures and the importance of teamwork relating to building maintenance and facilities management

Marks are awarded across three banded levels with an increasing amount of evidence required to meet the higher band three outcomes. These are clearly specified in the assessment marking table within the specification.

Marks are awarded based upon the depth of knowledge a student demonstrates in each of the focus areas. This means they could theoretically achieve top marks in one assessment focus and a score of nil in another. Assessment foci are marked in three bands: band 1 generally asks the student to 'briefly describe' or 'evaluate', band 2 asks for 'descriptions', band 3 asks for 'explanation and justification'. Assessment should be based on a 'best fit' approach to the grid.

This unit is assessed over three tasks as follows.

Learning Outcome 6.1: Know how sustainability affects the built environment

Students need to investigate the key focus of sustainability. In this task students conduct a role play in which they have been appointed as a consultant for a supermarket chain to produce a report on the sustainability of its growth and maintenance works.

This report should contain and describe the implications of sustainable decisions taken at the design stage to include, social, community, life cycle issues and environmental and economic impacts of developments.

What guidance will you give?

The use of a guest speaker would prove valuable. A suitable designer invited in to talk to the students would provide an ideal opportunity to view real live projects and discuss and interview the sustainable implications of such projects. The use of a major supermarkets design department as a resource would also prove valuable in focusing the students onto real design issues.

What should you look for in marking?

The student needs to briefly describe some sustainable design practices that could be used and would provide benefits for maintenance. The benefits of each must be expressed.

What gains higher assessment marks?

The student needs to define a range of sustainable practices clearly and with justification as to their use. An evaluation of the environmental impact upon current maintenance issues must be included.

How could students present the evidence?

The evidence needs to be presented in an A4 report word processed document. Any drawings or sketches should be no more that A3 size.

Learning Outcome 6.2: Be able to evaluate the contribution of the built environment to society and communities; Learning Outcome 6.3: Understand how the built environment can be improved to benefit individuals and communities

In this scenario the student is working as a journalist for a local newspaper. The newspaper editor has asked the student to produce a research article on property prices in your area. When the student undertakes the research for the report they must consider:

- An analysis of their built environment with regard to property prices, different types and how location and land prices have an affect on the type of property developed.

- How the built environment directly contributes to the local community and economy.

- The improvement of the physical built environment and how it has an affect upon the community with regard to the economic prosperity, spiritual, and emotional well being of individuals and communities.

What guidance will you give?

You can use your local newspaper to make this live and stimulating.

What should you look for in marking?

The student needs to describe the local property market and to include identifying factors that lead to sustainable communities. They also have to describe the way in which the built environment contributes to the creation of financial wealth. The ways in which the built environment can be improved, along with the benefits of development expansion must be considered with the key factors influencing development of sustainable communities.

What gains higher assessment marks?

The student needs to describe clearly in detail, and including an evaluation of, the local property market. A range of ways in which wealth is created should be evaluated. The student's description should clearly evaluate a range of ways in which the built environment can be improved, with a justification of developmental expansion.

How could students present the evidence?

Evidence is presented in the form of a newspaper article which is word processed or desk top published A4 size. No sketches or drawings larger than A3 should be included.

Learning Outcome 6.4: Understand the job roles, progression routes, occupational structures and the importance of teamwork relating to building maintenance and facilities management

In this task the student adopts the role of a consultant working within the construction recruitment sector. The department the student works in specializes in recruitment of facilities managers, building maintenance managers and property services. The student has been approached by a professional institution to provide a report of career options in their specialist area.

What guidance will you give?

The student will need to undertake some research on the various facilities, maintenance and property roles, career paths, jobs, and the role of the professional organisations.

What should you look for in marking?

The student needs to describe key job roles in the focused areas, including teamwork aspects. The role of the professional institutions needs to be described.

What gains higher assessment marks?

All of the key job roles need to be clearly described, including teamwork and progression paths within the focused key areas. A description of interactions with supervisory, technical and professional roles must be included. The professional institutions need to be explained and justified.

How could students present the evidence?

Information should be presented in the form of a written report. Drawings and sketches should be no larger than A3.

Delivering this unit

This unit has to be delivered around three set tasks within the specification. The first covers sustainability issues on a supermarket development. A site visit would be a good idea to gain experience of these issues.

Task two requires the student to consider the local property markets and here a local estate agent as a guest speaker would be advantageous to learning.

Task three examines the roles and responsibilities as a recruitment selector for construction.

The information in the student book for this unit is written in topics, each topic covering a particular learning outcome that relates to the awarding bodies specification. There are tasks at the end of each topic, some of which can be used to help with the production of the reports that have to be completed for this unit.

The activities in the ADR will reinforce students knowledge and can also be used to help build up evidence for the report.

Several of the activities are to reinforce knowledge learned in the student book and can be used to check understanding and be used as revision tools throughout this unit.

Integrating Functional Skills

Functional Skills can be applied throughout the topic both in the student book and the activities.

English – students will demonstrate their use of English throughout all the activities.

Speaking and listening – by contributing to discussions and making presentations and asking questions of outside speakers.

Reading – reading and understanding texts and using them to research and gather information.

Writing – communicating with others by using various written methods such as reports and letters.

ICT – students should be able to use ICT independently for a variety of tasks. They should be able to communicate and exchange information safely and responsibly, use the Internet for research and be able to present information in an effective and appropriate way such as producing text, images, tables, graphs and diagrams.

Personal, Learning and Thinking Skills

Some embedded uses of PLTS are incorporated in certain Edexcel assessment activities (see QCF unit summary inside the Edexcel unit specifications). However, use should be made of all opportunities to develop and enhance each students PLTS. Suitable opportunities will arise during the delivery and assessment activities for all of the elements of the Diploma. For example, the student may use their work experience to add to their PLTS experience and engagement. The development of the evidence portfolio on design will give the student the opportunity to use their personal and thinking skills in the solutions.

Linking to the Project

Some of the activities can be used as part of the students' project or can be the starting point towards gaining knowledge and information that will be developed should they wish to pursue this topic for their project. The relevant activities will point this out on the page.

Other useful resources

Work experience will further learning and understanding of how the sectors and services work together and these experiences will also aid work on the reports. In some circumstances this may be difficult to arrange therefore valuable insights can be obtained and primary evidence collected by inviting professionals in the sectors or services to visit and talk to the students as they can provide a stimulating input and enhance the learning of students.

Students should be encouraged to work in pairs or groups to gather information although they **must be aware** that they will need to produce an **individual report and project**.

Useful websites

- www.communities.gov.uk
- www.sustainabledesignnet.org.uk
- www.idea.gov.uk
- www.sustainable-development.gov.uk
- www.sustainable-development.gov.uk
- www.towards-sustainability.co.uk
- www.sustainablestuff.co.uk
- www.rics.org
- www.bifm.org.uk
- www.cibse.org

Insert Centre
Logo Here

Scheme of work   Title:

Level 2 Diploma Construction and the Built Environment
Unit 6: Value and use of the built environment: Communities

Academic year: ....

Edexcel unit leaning outcomes: Know how sustainability affects the built environment
Be able to evaluate the contribution of the built environment to society and communities
Understand how the built environment can be improved to benefit individuals and communities
Understand the job roles, progression routes, occupational structures and the importance of teamwork
relating to building maintenance and facilities management

Tutor/Lecturer(s) ....

Guided learning hours: **60 GLH (45 + 15)**

SB = Student Book
ADR = Assessment and Delivery Resource

GLH	Outcome/topic	Content	Student activity	Resources	Link to Learning objective
3	**The use of sustainable materials**	• The use of sustainable materials onsite • The benefits of using such materials • What is sustainable site practice? • Examples of SSP used on modern designs and construction projects • Advantages and disadvantages of each • Examples of key sustainable materials	• Students to discuss issues behind use of sustainable materials and record their thoughts • Identify some sustainable materials • Describe and discuss how sustainability affects the built environment • Web based research on sustainable materials • What are the benefits of using sustainable materials – team exercise and group summation • Guest speaker to discuss timber products • Students to create a marketing poster for a sustainable material	• Starter activity SB p170 • Activities SB p171 • Examples of sustainable materials from suppliers • ADR Activities p191	LO.6.1/1

#	Topic	Content	Activities	References
3	**Sustainable maintenance**	• What is sustainable maintenance? • What are the long term benefits in using this process? • Identify the benefits of sustainable maintenance • Examples on a typical project • Web based research on UK examples	• Students to contribute to discussion points on effect of non-maintenance • Team web research on sustainable practices on site, discuss examples in a full class discussion • Students to study their building and suggest upgrading areas with sustainable materials • Research suppliers and prepare a report on the benefits of materials	LO.6.1/1 • Starter activity SB p172 • Activities SB p173 • Personal learning and thinking skills SB p173 • Photographs of sustainable maintenance • ADR Activities p192
3	**Sustainability & the Built Environment**	• Link to Unit 4 Sustainable site practices • What can you change within the design and construction to help the environment • What are the sustainable benefits to a project? • What are the advantages for the projects resources	• Students link to ADR activities in Unit 4 • Discussion on sustainability on site • Group work on waste reduction measures on site	LO6.1/2 • ADR Unit 4
3	**Assessment Sessions**	• Students undertake the first session of assessment	• Learning Objective LO.6.1	LO.6.1 • Assessment portfolio/ assignment task sheet
3	**The property market**	• Public or private buildings • What is affordable housing? • What factors affect the property market • How does the property market meet the needs of a sustainable community?	• Starter activity: join teacher-led discussion on public and private housing • Look at a range of different types of property, discussing market issues • Investigate and feed back to class on first-time buyers, the market and what affects it • Produce a sales brochure to market a specified property • Research and categorise local property sales	LO.6.2/1 • Starter activity SB p182 • Activities SB 1, 2, 3 SB p182 • Functional skills SB p183 • ADR activities p198–9
3	**Influences on the property markets**	• Discussion on drawing out the principal factors that lead to a sustainable community • What affects or influences these factors – e.g. economy • Location and geographical factors • Introduction on the CBE and the creation of wealth	• Students participate in discussions, contribute to a mind map on possible influences • Research local property market and prepare a report on influences on property prices, visiting mortgage company websites and local estate agents. Work in teams to prepare a report. • Q+A session on the construction economy of the UK	LO.6.2/1 • Starter activity SB p184 • Activities SB p185 • Personal learning and thinking skills SB p184 • Functional skills SB p184 • ADR Activities 200–1

No	Topic	Learning content	Delivery	Activities	LO ref
3	**Construction and the economy**	• What key areas the construction sector covers • How construction contributes to the national economy • How construction & built environment contributes to the local economy • How it contributes to local economies	• Tutor-led discussion on how the construction industry responds when the economy slows • Join tutor-led discussion on the construction industries' contribution to local and national economies • Research and report on the growth areas in the construction industry over the past five years • Write a brief report on the key influences and employment areas in construction locally • Students to write out their impression and understanding of how the economy develops	• Starter activity SB p176 • Activities 1, 2, 3 SB p176 • ADR activities p1194–5	LO.6.2/2
3	**Assessment Sessions**	• Students undertake the second session of assessment	• Learning Objective LO.6.2	• Assessment portfolio/ assignment task sheet	LO.6.2
3	**Housing and the economy**	• The schemes which are available to support people in buying homes who cannot afford it • How house prices affect the economy • What causes land to be expensive	• Students mindmap different types of homes, including values and other economic factors • Students to research affordability of property for a range of incomes before discussion on affordability and access • Why do house prices effect the economy with thinking time and discussion in groups • Create a guide to home buying for a first time buyer	• Starter activity SB p178 • Functional skills SB p178 • Personal learning and thinking skills SB p179 • Activities 1, 2, 3 SB p178 • ADR activities p196	LO.6.3/1
3	**Housing in the UK**	• The different types of housing available • Housing Factors influencing the development of sustainable communities • What regeneration means • Reusing buildings for housing	• Discuss with partner and record why people may choose different types of housing and why • Feedback to group on discussion • Research different types of housing, regeneration and prior use, using the internet and local resources. Feedback on findings • Carry out a survey on types of housing and identify a local building that could be re-used	• Starter activity SB p180 • Activities 1, 2, 3 SB p180 • ADR activities p197	LO.6.3/2
3	**Improving the built environment**	• Why we should seek to improve the built environment • How improving the built environment contributes to our well-being • How improving the built environment can aid economic prosperity • Methods to improve our environment • Education	• Tutor-led discussion of student's environment and the feeling of wellbeing • Students to write a report on enhancing their built environment and feedback to rest of group • Social, moral and spiritual aspects of the built environment • Discuss in pairs social and community issues in areas that need improving	• Starter activity SB p186 • Activities 1, 2, 3 SB p187 • ADR activities p202	LO.6.3/1

	Topic	Content	Activities	Resources	LO ref
3	**Refurbishment and conservation**	• What refurbishing a building involves • How conservation matters to a structure • How can this improve the environment • Local examples • National Examples • What a listed building or structure is	• Tutor-led discussion on the issues surrounding refurbishment or demolition of a building • Prepare a report on a chosen historical building • Join in whole-class discussion and tutor-led guidance on the processes of refurbishment and conservation – note-taking • Research possible refurbishment projects in your local area	• Starter activity SB p188 • Activities 1, 2 SB p189 • Functional skills SB p188 • ADR activities p203	LO.6.3/1
3	**Sustainable communities**	• What the benefits are of living in a sustainable community • Why the government promotes sustainable communities • What impact a sustainable community can have in the wider world	• Students discuss in groups the changes that can influence sustainability in the community • Tutor-led discussion of the benefits of living in sustainable communities • Students research components of sustainable communities, including local issues • Working in pairs, discuss the research carried out and the benefits of living in a sustainable community • Role-play in teams preparing answers for questions related to a housing development	• Starter activity SB p174 • Activities 1, 2, 3 SB p174 • Functional skills SB p175 • Personal learning and thinking skills SB p175 • ADR activities p193	LO.6.3/2
3	**Assessment Sessions**	• Students undertake the third session of assessment	• Learning Objective LO.6.3	• Assessment portfolio/ assignment task sheet	LO.6.3
3	**The responsibility of maintaining the built environment 1**	• Introduction to the job roles that maintain the built environment • The five categories of roles for people who create the built environment: craft, technical, professional, supervisory, management • The roles and their specialist skills • The different organisations that professionals belong to	• Discuss the main roles and responsibilities in maintaining a building and why these need to done, guessing the classification of role • Tutor-led discussion: more detail on the different roles within the construction industry • Investigate leading professional institutions and what services they perform	• Starter activity SB p192 • Activities 1, 2, 3 SB p192 • ADR activities p205	LO.6.4/1
3	**The responsibility of maintaining the built environment 2**	• What benefits does maintenance bring to the community as a whole? • Identification of the factors that affect maintenance • Link to Unit 7	• Students discuss the maintenance of the environment they are in now • Identify what factors affect this maintenance • Q+A session in teams as to the benefits of maintenance	• ADR activities p205	LO.6.3/1 LO.6.4/1

3	**The surveyor's role in maintenance and construction**	• The different types of surveyor • What makes a good surveyor? • The special equipment you need for surveying • The role of the surveyor in facilities management	• In pairs, discuss what the Egyptians might have used as early surveying techniques • Discuss different types of surveyor, their roles and equipment • Students investigate linear dimensions and types of surveyors writing reports to cover these • Students select and investigate a run-down building in local area; write report outlining the defects of this building	• Starter activity SB p190 • Activities 1, 2, 3 SB 191 • ADR Activities p204	LO.6.4/1
3	**Professional Institutions**	• Tutor describes the occupational structures of team members within building maintenance • The role of the professional institutions • Building Maintenance Associations • Link to LO 5.4	• Students draw up a typical structure for a large maintenance team • Discuss role of RIBA, RICS & CIOB in maintenance	• Outline diagram for structure to fill in by students	LO.6.4/2
3	**Assessment Sessions**	• Students undertake the forth session of assessment	• Learning Objective LO.6.3	• Assessment portfolio/ assignment task sheet	LO.6.4
3	**Assessment Sessions**	• Students undertake the fifth session of assessment • Plenary to complete all outstanding assessments	• All Learning Objective LO's	• Assessment portfolio/ assignment task sheet	All LO's

Level 2 Diploma in Construction and the Built Environment

Lesson plan 1
Unit 6: Value and use of the built environment: Community – housing in the UK

Centre name: **Tutor/lecturer(s):**

Aims & objectives

• To consider what types of housing are available in the UK

SB = Student Book 1
ADR = Assessment and Delivery Resource

Learning objectives   **Total lesson time:** 90 minutes

• All students should understand what is meant by the different types of housing LO6.3
• Most students will be able to define them LO 6.3

Timings reflect one typical session within the GLH block of 3 hours allocated in the SOW

Timing/ Content	Tutor activity	Student activity	Resources	Individualised activity/differentiation	Personal Learning and Thinking Skills	Functional Skills
5 mins Welcome students and Register	Check health and safety of the room. Take a register	Enter room in accordance with normal procedures and settle quickly	Register			
10 mins Starter	Who lives in a house like this? – starter activity. Write feedback up on board to reflect the thoughts of the students	In pairs discussion regarding the different types of housing available and why it is needed. Feedback to tutor – each group to feedback opinions	Paper if needed to note down feedback	Feedback allows students to share ideas. Tutor to ensure students remain on task and prompt groups if struggling with concept	Effective participators – able to join in discussion. Team workers able to manage input from others in group and encourage discussions	

Time / Topic	Tutor activity	Student activity	Resources	Differentiation / support	Skills
10 mins Types of housing Regeneration and reuse	Explanation of different types of housing available	Refer to table in p180 of SB Note taking	SB p180, note-taking grids	Direction for less able students to use note-taking grids to organise thoughts and explanation	Students work on note taking and English skills
40 mins	Outline tasks – research into types of housing, community regeneration and buildings being reused	Completion of Activities 1, 2 and 3. 1. Copying a complete table on different types of housing – using internet research 2. Research on community regeneration 3. Finding buildings that have had a prior use	SB activities p180 Computer suite for research Large sheets of paper to record results of all three tasks	Tutor to ensure that students remain on task, and prompt groups if struggling with concept	Functional skills – English and ICT – using ICT for research, presenting information clearly using appropriate language
10 mins	Feedback – what have you found out?	Students to give feedback to class and tutor	Area to display findings	Assistance if required to aid feedback	English skills through presentation
10 mins Textbook activity for extension or suggested homework task	Explanation of ADR activities – carrying out a survey of housing, find a building that could be reused and sketch the change you could make	Students to record homework/extension activity and ask questions to aid understanding	Homework planner ADR p197	Additional support for students who need concepts behind research outlined	
5 mins Plenary	Review of learning objectives	Q&A session to reflect on learning	What are the different types of housing? What does regeneration mean? What type of buildings may be re used for housing and why?		Reflective students – consider what they have learnt to secure learning

Level 2 Diploma in Construction and the Built Environment

Lesson plan 2

Unit 6: Value and use of the built environment: Communities – Housing and the economy

Centre name: Tutor/lecturer(s):

Aims & objectives

- To consider how the housing market affects the economy

SB = Student Book 1
ADR = Assessment and Delivery Resource

Learning objectives

- All students should understand how housing effects the economy LO.6.2/2
- Most students will have considered how this may affect them later in their lives LO.6.2/2

Timings reflect one typical session within the GLH block of 3 hours allocated in the SOW

Total lesson time: 180 minutes

Timing/ Content	Tutor activity	Student activity	Resources	Individualised activity/differentiation	Personal learning and thinking skills	Functional skills
5 mins Welcome students and register	Check health and safety of the room Take a register	Enter room in accordance with normal procedures and settle quickly	Register			
10 mins Starter activity	Introduce the links between the built environment, money and society	Consider and jot down thoughts on how much they think their own home is worth, how much a mortgage would be for it and how much they would have to earn to be able to afford it	Notepaper Starter activity SB p178	Less able students to be allowed greater time and support whilst thinking – use questions and prompts to initiate ideas.		

Time	Tutor activity	Student activity	Resources	Notes	Skills
25 mins Affordability	Outline affordability task	Look at one of the major banks or building societies and use their mortgage calculators to see how much you could borrow if you earned the stated incomes	Internet access	Students to find a major bank's mortgage calculator – tutor could suggest websites. Tutor could carry out one of the incomes as an example	Students use calculations to increase mathematics abilities. IT skills – independent internet research can be used for more able students
10 mins	Start a discussion on affordability and access	Join in Q&A session looking at different schemes available to aid affordability			Debate to encourage independent thinking
15 mins	Go through with students the reasons why housing affects the economy	In groups, discuss the reasons listed in the SB p178–9	Reasons why housing affects the economy SB p178–9	Prompt groups with questions	Debate to encourage independent thinking
10 mins	Tutor-led discussion on reasons why housing affects the economy	Give feedback from groups to tutor			
80 mins Textbook activity and extension	Introduce Activities 1, 2 and 3 from SB. Encourage students to work in groups to complete the activities and debate their ideas	Students to complete activities 1, 2 and 3 from SB, using Internet and other resources	Activities 1, 2 and 3 SB p178. Internet access. Access to computer software to complete Activity 2	Support individuals by outcome, placing less able students with more confident. Encourage debate and sharing of ideas between students.	Independent enquirers – investigation and research. Self managers – working towards organisation of information. Functional skills – ICT
20 mins	Lead Q&A on activity tasks	Group feeds results of activities back to tutor	Activities 1, 2 and 3 SB p178 Paper		
5 mins	Plenary	Review of learning objectives	Q&A session to reflect on learning	What schemes are available to support people in buying homes who cannot afford this? How do house prices affect the economy? What causes land to be expensive?	Reflective students – consider what they have learnt to secure learning

6.1   The use of sustainable materials

Student Book
pp 170–171

1   Identify which of these materials are a sustainable source. Ring your answers.

   ■   cement

   ■   wool insulation

   ■   concrete

   ■   cedar cladding

   ■   foam flooring insulation

   ■   clay roof tiles

   ■   hardwood external door

   ■   drainage gravel

   ■   crushed brick hardcore

2   Timber is a natural product that can be grown, managed and harvested, then replanted. It is therefore a fully sustainable material, apart from processing and transport costs.

   Using the Internet, find out what certification schemes are available in the UK to ensure that the timber that we use is from a sustainable source.

3   Locate a building that is run down and in need of possible demolition in or near to your town, village or city. By taking a look at this from the outside, identify five products that could be recycled from the demolition of this structure.

6.2 Sustainable maintenance

**Student Book
pp 172–173**

1 A new housing estate is going to be constructed near to where you live. You are on 10 days work experience with the company that has won the tender to construct the houses. Your manager has set you a small task to complete.

 She tells you that the rainwater systems on site could use one of the following:

 ■ seamless aluminium guttering

 ■ uPVC guttering

 ■ timber guttering.

 Your task is to find a supplier for each material, and find out the life span of the material, so a comparison can be made.

 Which material would you recommend to the manager for its long-term sustainability?

2 Medium density fibreboard (MDF) is a versatile material often used for constructing cupboards and fitted furniture in homes, and as a replacement material for maintenance – but it has its problems.

 What are the problems associated with MDF? Investigate these, looking at the material as a sustainable and environmentally friendly product.

3 Using Google Earth and the internet, find an example of a green roof planted on a building. Try to find out more about this building – where it is, what sort of property it is, what the area is like, etc.

 Establish five benefits of using such a roof.

 Use your findings to help you construct a marketing leaflet for a new green roofing company forming in the UK. Use a photograph of the roof you've found as the central feature of your leaflet.

6.3   Sustainable communities

Student Book
pp 174–175

1   You have been asked to read the following statements prior to them being released in a marketing campaign for a local housing development. Check whether these are true or false. Where they are false, provide the correct statement on that subject.

- The properties that we are selling have their own waste incinerators.

- The toilet system uses rainwater to flush.

- Cycle paths are on every road.

- There are no open green spaces.

- Sustainable materials are used in our designs.

- Wind turbines are used to produce water.

2   Work in teams of three. Imagine your team is working for a local housing developer. One of you is a sustainability expert, one a construction expert and the other a press officer.

The housing developer is keen to make all their future developments sustainable communities. There is a great need for this type of housing in the area where you live, and they want you to help prepare some answers to questions that local residents, council workers and community association members are bound to ask.

In your roles, help prepare the answers to the following questions:

- What will the developer do to make sure these homes are affordable?

- How will recycled materials be used in the construction?

- What public transport facilities will there be from this development?

- How will the members of these new communities be able to have their say in local matters concerning the environment?

6.4   Construction and the economy

Student Book
pp 176–177

1   This text gives an overview of the effect of the construction industry on the UK economy. Complete the text by filling in the missing words.

The construction industry is a large employer within the UK and contributes a large percentage towards the _____ of the UK. When a building is _____ and completed also contributes to _____ in general. While the building is being constructed it provides _____ and _____ for the workforce.

wages   economy   constructed   employment   society

2   The UK construction industry works for a number of markets within the UK and provides a number of services to its customers. The following article taken from the Contract Journal Webpage illustrates some of the UK construction markets. After you have read it, answer these questions.

News round-up 2006

British Land has become the latest victim of the credit crunch as it pulled out of selling part of its £1.6billion shopping centre in Meadowhall, Sheffield. The company had been marketing their 75% stake since May 2006, but stated "uncertainty in financial markets" had dictated its decision.

Ikea has begun selling flat-pack homes from its outlet in Gateshead. Designed by Skanska, these timber framed homes cost up to £150,000 and are only available to those earning £15,000 to £35,000 a year.

HMRC have warned contractors that they face fines unless their monthly returns are filed on time, as well as returns for the amnesty period of the last six months.

The Bank of England has decided to keep interest rates on hold at 5.75% despite the fall of house prices by 0.6% in the past year. The Bank is said to be looking for further evidence that the housing market is "softening".

- How as the situation in the economy affected British Land? What might the local affect be of this decision?

- Why might the Ikea timber houses only be available to those within a fixed income band?

- What did the Bank of England mean when they say they were waiting for the housing market to "soften"?

3   The economy of construction is strongly linked to the growth of the overall UK economy. When this does well, businesses invest in new projects that require buildings.

■   When the economy is growing and buoyant, how does this affect construction?

■   What happens when we enter a recession?

■   Are there plenty of job opportunities in a recession? How are employers and employees in construction affected?

■   If our economy slows down, can UK construction companies work abroad in European countries?

Using your answers to these questions, write a few paragraphs to explain your understanding of the links between the state of the economy and the construction industry.

6.5   Housing and the economy

**Student Book
pp 178–179**

1   There are many reasons why housing affects the economy. Try and match the reasons up with the correct statements.

Lower interest rates allow the consumer to spend less on interest payments and therefore allow them to spend more on goods and services including houses. Higher interest rates mean that people have to spend more money on interest, and therefore become more cautious about spending on goods and services.	Location – workplace
If the housing has this, people can commute to work if they cannot afford to live near to work.	Cheaper housing
Many people buy in an area because of this, but it depends on the availability of transport.	House prices
If these rise, people can increase spending. This is because they can remortgage or take a bigger loan out against the value of their property. Higher spending can then contribute to economic growth.	Accommodation for essential workers
These people are needed in all areas and often schemes are put in place to help them.	Rates of interest
Where people work, spend and have leisure time is dependent on housing being close to these areas. If they do not live close by, they may spend elsewhere, which affects the local economy.	Location – relative to transport

2   Carry out some research on land prices in the UK. Check out local and national estate agents' websites to compare the price of land in different areas of the country.

6.6   Housing in the UK

**Student Book
pp 180–181**

1 Carry out a survey to find out what types of housing there are in your local area. Use a table similar to the one below to record your results. You could also turn your results into graphs using a spreadsheet package.

Style of housing in the UK	Number of homes
Terraced	
Semi-detached	
Detached	
Bungalow	
Flat	
Apartment	
Barn Conversion	
Other	

2 Look at a building that is not currently in use in your local area. Decide how you could re-use it. Draw out a rough plan of how you may change the use of the building.

6.7   The property market

Student Book
pp 182–183

1   Get hold of a copy of the weekly property guide delivered with a commercial local newspaper.

Have a look through it for rental properties. Complete the following table for four different types of property you find.

Type of property	Description/features	Rental value

2   The first time buyer in the UK is struggling to get on the first rung of the property ladder. There are several ways in which this can be achieved. State whether the following are true or false:

   ■ It is impossible to get on the first rung of the ladder

   ■ You can get a lifetime mortgage

   ■ Often you need to rent first in order to save a deposit

   ■ Lenders don't like first time buyers and don't offer special deals

3   Investigate any housing association working within an area near you. Find out the answers to these questions.

   ■ Is the housing association a charity?

   ■ Does the association provide supported housing?

   ■ Is housing available specifically for the elderly?

   Write down any other information that you think makes this association a good thing, or particularly well suited to your local area.

6.8   Influences on the property market

Student Book
pp 184–185

1   Get a copy of the local paper for your area and look through the property guide. Examine the different types of property available for sale in your area, then answer these questions.

    ■ What types of commercial property are for sale?

    ■ How many different types of private property are for sale?

    ■ Are there any public properties for sale?

    ■ Is there any property to rent?

2   Match the correct factor to the current property market situation.

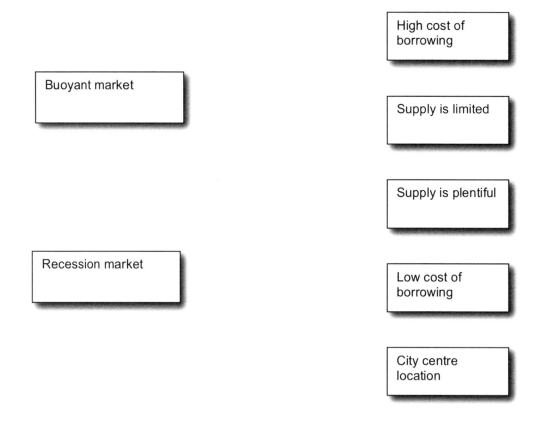

3   Using the internet, research the state of the property market over the last few years. Has it grown? Produce a graph showing the percentage increases/decreases over the last year, or for a period as current as you can find. Write a few notes on what the graph shows

4   Locate an area of available land near to your place of residence. This is going to be used to develop a new set of houses that will be a low cost option for first time buyers.

Identify at least five factors that will influence the 'saleability' of these new homes, and use them to complete the list below. One example is done for you.

1   The cost of borrowing

2   _____

3   _____

4   _____

5   _____

6   _____

6.9   Improving the built environment

**Student Book
pp 186–187**

1   Look at the built environment around the area where you live or where you go to school. What could be improved? Write a report to state the things that could be changed and say how each change would improve the built environment.

2   The following phrases are often used when talking about how we might improve the built environment. Try to write your own definition of these terms. Once you have had a go yourself, check them with a dictionary or on the internet.

Bring the house up to current and future standards	Better insulated
More desirable	Refurbishment
Modification	Eco-friendly
Changes to meet future needs	More efficient

6.10   Refurbishment and conservation

Student Book
pp 188–189

1   A local two-storey office block in your town centre is undergoing a refurbishment contract. The building is over 50 years old, and when the work is finished, this will entirely upgrade the surrounding area.

What aspects of such a building would be replaced in a refurbishment? Make a list of at least four.

_____

_____

_____

_____

_____

_____

2   Conservation often involves historic buildings. What particular items would you consider conserving on a historic building that would not be considered on a refurbishment? List four.

_____

_____

_____

_____

_____

6.11   The role of the surveyor

Student Book
pp 190–191

1   You have just completed your construction qualification and are starting your first job, as an assistant to the building surveyor in a local office. You have been asked to select the equipment for a survey. From the following list, circle the correct equipment for a roof void survey.

■   folding ladders

■   manhole lifting keys

■   torch

■   dust mask

■   level and staff

■   plumb line

■   damp meter

■   camera

2   You have been asked to look at a detached property for a valuation on a loan in order for the application to be processed. The property is only about 30 years old and is constructed using traditional methods.

■   What items would be considered when deciding the value of the property?

■   For what defects might you hold back monies for repairs?

■   How long do you think would be spent on such a survey?

6.12   The responsibility of maintaining the built environment

Student Book
pp 192–193

1   Match the following roles to the correct descriptions by drawing lines

Operative	A person who would set out a building
Craft	A person who may design or quantify the building
Technical	A person who would undertake the manual labouring role on site
Professional	A person who has a trade skill

2   The following are the associations of the professional roles: CIOB (Chartered Institute of Building) and RICS (Royal Institute of Chartered Surveyors). Work in pairs. Each visit the website of one of these institutes and, between you, answer the following questions:

■ How many years has the RICS been formed?

■ How many members has it got?

■ How many countries does it cover?

■ How many branches of the CIOB are there?

■ How many members does the CIOB have?

■ When was its Royal Charter granted?

Once you have done your research, come back together in your pairs and tell your partner what you have learnt about the institute you chose. Which do you think is better? Discuss in your pairs.

3   You are considering entering the civil engineering profession. Does this profession have an institute? Find out, and then answer these questions:

■ What services does it provide for its members?

■ Can anybody join the institute?

■ What qualifications do you need to join this professional body?

■ Can you use letters after your name?

7

Value and Use of the Built Environment: Facilities Management

Links with other units

Level 1
- Unit 5: Value and use of the built environment

Level 3
- Unit 7: Value and use of the built environment: Protecting and maintaining

Topics covered	Edexcel unit learning outcomes
Maintenance	Know about maintenance of the built environment
Maintenance services	Understand how services are provided
Management provision	Be able to analyse facilities management provision.

How this unit will be assessed

Assessment is based on the student being able to demonstrate that they have met three learning outcomes. These are:

LO 7.1 Know about maintenance of the built environment

LO 7.2 Understand how services are provided

LO 7.3 Be able to analyse facilities management provision

Marks are awarded across three banded levels with an increasing amount of evidence required to meet the higher band three outcomes. These are clearly specified in the assessment marking table within the specification.

Marks are awarded based upon the depth of knowledge a student demonstrates in each of the focus areas. This means they could theoretically achieve top marks in one assessment focus and a score of nil in another. Assessment foci are marked in three bands: band 1 generally asks the student to 'briefly describe' or 'evaluate', band 2 asks for 'descriptions', band 3 asks for 'explanation and justification'. Assessment should be based on a 'best fit' approach to the grid.

This assessment is best based around a suitable construction project activity. Access to a suitable organisation that uses facilities management within its strategy needs to be provided as a resource for the student to focus upon. This organisation could be a hospital, factory, university or shopping centre but should be large enough to provide a wide range of facilities services. The student acts in the role of an assistant to the managing director who has asked the student to report on their facilities management provision. The three learning outcomes are woven into three focus areas that must be included into a report. Each of these is as follows.

Learning Outcome 7.1: Know about maintenance of the built environment

The student will need to explain the need to maintain the built environment. The processes involved must be explored. Design decisions and their affect on current maintenance also need to be identified.

What guidance will you give?

The student can look closely at the organisation selected by the tutor, which will act as a physical prompt to identify the need to maintain, manage and protect the built environment. This should cover all the basic criteria for band one assessment. If access to the organisation is not obtained then suitable web based built environment opportunities may be present.

What should you look for in marking?

A description of the key processes involved in the protection, maintenance and management of a structure.

What gains higher assessment marks?

The student needs to clearly identify the key processes, and discuss and justify the purposes of each with identification of the benefits of these.

How could students present the evidence?

The evidence needs to be presented in an A4 word processed report. Any drawings or sketches should be no more than A3 size.

Learning Outcome 7.2: Understand how services are provided

What guidance will you give?

The student will need access to the managerial side of the organisation so that they can gain information on the way in which facilities management is organised and arranged within a large organisation. The impact of such services also has to be identified with regard to the lifespan of the building. The student will need to identify the social and economic benefits that such management brings to the organisation and the wider community.

What should you look for in marking?

The student will need to describe the different ways there are of organising and managing the delivered services for the organisation. The student needs to identify and describe the impact of such services on the potential lifespan of the building. The social and economic benefits of delivering such services also need to be described.

What gains higher assessment marks?

The methods employed to organise and manage need to be clearly described along with specifying a broad range of delivered services. The economic and social benefits need to be discussed in detail.

How could students present the evidence?

The evidence needs to be presented in an A4 word processed report. Any drawings or sketches should be no more than A3 size.

Learning Outcome 7.3: Be able to analyze facilities management provision

What guidance will you give?

The student needs to undertake an analysis of the companies' facilities management provision. Here confidentiality must be carefully considered and a relationship must be developed with a suitable company that will support such an educational partnership.

What should you look for in marking?

The student needs to briefly describe some of the key facilities management provisions in the company and include the benefits of each of these.

What gains higher assessment marks?

The key features need to be clearly described with an evaluation of the benefits of each considering alternative approaches.

How could students present the evidence?

The evidence needs to be presented in an A4 word processed report. Any drawings or sketches should be no more than A3 size.

Delivering this unit

This unit is best delivered around an activity based assessment. A scenario facilities management exemplar will be given by the tutor. This should be a local organisation that the student can relate to.

The information in the student book for this unit is written in topics, each topic covering a particular learning outcome that relates to the awarding bodies specification. There are tasks at the end of each topic, some of which can be used to help with the production of the reports that have to be completed for this unit.

The activities in the ADR will reinforce students knowledge and can also be used to help build up evidence for the report.

Several of the activities are to reinforce knowledge learned in the student book and can be used to check understanding and be used as revision tools throughout this unit.

Integrating Functional Skills

Functional Skills can be applied throughout the topic both in the student book and the activities.

English – students will demonstrate their use of English throughout all the activities.

Speaking and listening – by contributing to discussions and making presentations and asking questions of outside speakers.

Reading – reading and understanding texts and using them to research and gather information.

Writing – communicating with others by using various written methods such as reports and letters.

ICT – students should be able to use ICT independently for a variety of tasks. They should be able to communicate and exchange information safely and responsibly, use the Internet for research and be able to present information in an effective and appropriate way such as producing text, images, tables, graphs and diagrams.

Personal, Learning and Thinking Skills

Some embedded uses of PLTS are incorporated in certain Edexcel assessment activities (see QCF unit summary inside the Edexcel unit specifications). However, use should be made of all opportunities to develop and enhance each student's PLTS. Suitable opportunities will arise during the delivery and assessment activities for all of the elements of the Diploma. For example, the student may use their work experience to add to their PLTS experience and engagement. The development of the evidence portfolio on design will give the student the opportunity to use their personal and thinking skills in the solutions.

Linking to the Project

Some of the activities can be used as part of the students' project or can be the starting point towards gaining knowledge and information that will be developed should they wish to pursue this topic for their project. The relevant activities will point this out on the page.

Other useful resources

Work experience will further learning and understanding of how the sectors and services work together and these experiences will also aid work on the reports. In some circumstances this may be difficult to arrange therefore valuable insights can be obtained and primary evidence collected by inviting professionals in the sectors or services to visit and talk to the students as they can provide a stimulating input and enhance the learning of students.

Students should be encouraged to work in pairs or groups to gather information although they **must be aware** that they will need to produce an **individual report and project**.

Useful websites

- www.bifm.org.uk
- www.nationalgrid.com
- www.nationalgrid.com/uk/electricity
- www.fmassociation.org.uk
- www.fmug.org.uk

　　　　　209

Insert Centre
Logo Here

Scheme of work   Title: Centre Name:

Level 2 Diploma Construction and the Built Environment

Unit 7: Value and use of the built environment: facilities management

Academic year: ....

Edexcel unit learning outcome: Know about maintenance of the built environment

Understand how services are provided

Be able to analyse facilities management provision

Tutor/Lecturer(s) ....

SB = Student Book

ADR = Assessment and Delivery Resource

Guided learning hours: 60 GLH (45 + 15)

GLH	Outcome/topic	Content	Student activity	Resources	Link to Learning objective
3.5	**Maintenance**	• Why properties need to be maintained regularly • What a defect liability contract is • The sorts of defects that can occur within the first twelve months of a building being completed • The impact of design decisions on maintenance	• Quick fire questions – three reasons why student's homes have to be regularly maintained • Tutor-led discussion on what the two terms liable and defect mean • Students research liability periods and possible repairs • Prepare report on role of architect • Research possible maintenance issues in a building with a special function • Students role-play drawing up a maintenance contract	• Starter activity SB p198 • Functional skills SB p198 • Personal learning and thinking skills SB p198 • Activities 1, 2, 3 SB p198 • ADR activities p220, 222	LO.7.1/1

No.	Topic	Content	Delivery	Resources	LO
3.5	Maintenance	The major processes involved in the protection, maintenance and management of the built environment; Facilitates support on presentations	Students in teams discuss each of the roles; Produce a small presentation on each in teams; Tutor divides group into teams to explore the three areas	PowerPoint; Internet and ICT	LO.7.1/1
2	Maintenance	View and feedback on presentations	Students present findings; Answer any questions presented by tutor; Feedback to peers	ICT	LO.7.1/1
3	Site Visit Preparation	Prepare a site visit to an appropriate employer that is involved within facilities management; Prepare students for the assessment tasks; Undertake research on employer	Read and understand the assessment tasks; Participate in the site visit; Undertake the research on the employer or company; Develop the questions to ask the company; Ensure full understanding of the tasks	Site visit	
1	Assessment Sessions	Students undertake the first session of assessment; Prepare students for what this outcome requires	Learning Objective LO 7.1/1; Fully understand the evidence required	Assessment portfolio/ assignment task sheet	LO.7.1
3.5	How facilities services are provided	The ways in which maintenance can be delivered; Examples of delivery and benefits of each; The financial and social contribution of such services to the built environment	Tutor-led discussion on economic issues in maintenance supply; Take notes on the delivery of maintenance; Study the social/economic impact of a particular building that has undergone maintenance in the local area; Research the benefits of contracting out facilities management; Produce a mock advert for a facilities manager	Starter activity SB p200; Functional skills SB p200; Activities SB p201; ADR Activities p221	LO.7.2/1
8	Site Visit	A planned site visit to a company that has a wide range of maintenance delivered; Pre-planned visit; Risk Assessments	Students participate in visit; Take notes for assessment	Transport; Question sheets	LO.7.2/1

No.	Topic	Content	Activities	Resources	LO
3	**Lifecycle costing and sustainability**	• How buildings have their own lifecycle • What is lifecycle costing? • The benefits of taking a holistic approach to building	• Students to prepare own ideas of the stages of a building's life stages before tutor-led discussion on lifecycle costing and the benefits • Study a local development and review lifecycle costing implications • Role-play the briefing of an architect and proposing a development to a local authority • Research how lifecycle costs can be reduced	• Starter activity SB p206 • Activities 1, 2, 3 SB p207 • Personal learning and thinking SB p206 • ADR activities p225	LO 7.2/2
3	**Property services**	• What the area of property services entails • What the social and economic benefits of asset management are • What differences there are between public and private investment	• Students to record thoughts on property ownership before a group discussion on property services and asset management • Tutor-led discussion on social and economic aspects • Internet research to investigate how funding can be obtained for a new community project • Do internet research on finding funding on areas in UK with funding assistance and private investors • Research different types of property services available	• Starter activity SB p208 • Activities 1, 2, 3 SB p209 • Functional skills SB p209 • Computer suite for research • Internet research record sheet • ADR activities p226	LO.7.2/3
1	**Assessment Sessions**	• Students undertake the second session of assessment • Prepare students for outcome requires	• Learning Objective LO 7.1/1 • Fully understand the evidence required	• Assessment portfolio/assignment task sheet	LO 7.2
3.5	**Planned maintenance**	• The three principles of maintenance • What property maintenance can involve • The benefits of property maintenance • Social and economic benefits of using managed services • The benefits to the sustainable community as a whole	• Tutor-led discussion on the consequences of avoiding planned maintenance • Discuss three principles of maintenance • Identify three buildings that need maintenance and suggest why this might not yet have taken place • Research CDM and its implications to complete case study • Produce a check-list for planned maintenance	• Starter activity SB p204 • Activities 1, 2 SB p204 • Case study SB p204 • Computer suite for research • Internet research record sheet • ADR activities p223-4	LO.7.3

	Topic	Content	Activities	Resources	LO
3	**Facilities management provision**	• What the term 'facilities' covers • What a facilities manager does • How a facilities manager obtains the services needed	• Discussion in pairs on what facilities have to be managed leading into whole-class discussion and feedback • Join tutor-led discussion on the role of a facilities manager • Research in pairs other roles under the title Facilities manager • Prepare questions for interviewing estates manager at your school • Join whole-class discussion on who does the work and monitoring performance • Select a specific organisation to research • Prepare a document briefing improved performance for a contractor	• Starter activity SB p196 • Personal skills activity SB p196 • Activities 1, 2, 3 SB p197 • Functional skills SB p197 • Computer suite for research • Internet research record sheet • ADR activities p219	LO 7.3
5	**Assessment Sessions**	• Students undertake the final session of assessment preparation • Prepare students for what this outcome requires	• Learning Objective LO 7.1/1 • Fully understand the evidence required	• Assessment portfolio/assignment task sheet	LO.7. 3
3	**Report outline**	• Introduction to assessment report • Teacher to outline an organisation that is involved in facilities management • Describe proposal, plans, elevations and site layout drawing • Description of the managed services within the company	• Discuss report outline • Study drawings and plans • Make notes on key points of report	• Proposal outline • Plans for development • Site layout drawings • Examples of managed services and photographs	LO 7.1 LO 7.2 LO 7.3
2	**Experiential learning**	• Presentation techniques • Web search criteria • Three areas of assessment	• Research the need to maintain, processes involved and decisions made • Research how services are provided • Research analysing facilities management provision • Produce a presentation in groups on the above areas	• Internet access • Access to computer and PowerPoint • List of useful websites	LO 7.1 LO 7.2 LO 7.3
3	**Know about the processes in maintaining the built environment**	• Presentations given by groups to rest of class and feedback given	• In groups give presentations • Other students to make notes on note-taking grid • Self and peer assessment grids to be filled in by audience	• ICT, computer and reporter • Note-taking grid • Self and peer assessment grids	LO 7.1 LO 7.2 LO 7.3

3	**Understand how services are provided**	• Guidance on this section of the report	• Make notes on this section • Write this section of the report	• Mark scheme • Computer access • Internet access for further research	LO 7.1 LO 7.2 LO 7.3
3	**Understand how services are provided**	• Guidance on this section of the report	• Make notes on this section • Write this section of the report	• Mark scheme • Computer access • Internet access for further research	LO 7.1 LO 7.2 LO 7.3
3	**Be able to analyse facilities management provision**	• Guidance on this section of the report	• Make notes on this section • Write this section of the report	• Mark scheme • Computer access • Internet access for further research	LO 7.1 LO 7.2 LO 7.3

Level 2 Diploma in Construction and the Built Environment

Lesson plan 1

Unit 7: Value and use of the built environment: Facilities management – Lifecycle costing and sustainability 1

Centre name:

Tutor/lecturer(s):

Aims & objectives

- To consider what the lifecycle of a building is

SB = Student Book 1
ADR = Assessment and Delivery Resource

Total lesson time: 90 minutes

Learning objectives

- To understand what is meant by the lifecycle of a building LO.7.2/2
- Be able to carry out an investigation into sustainable lifecycle costs LO.7.2/3

Timings reflect one typical session within the GLH block of 3 hours allocated in the SOW

Timing/ Content	Tutor activity	Student activity	Resources	Individualised activity/differentiation	Personal learning and thinking skills	Functional skills
5 mins Welcome students and register	Check health and safety of the room. Take a register	Enter room in accordance with normal procedures and settle quickly	Register			
15 mins Starter activity	Starter activity – Can a building have a lifecycle?	Write down ideas about the stages of a buildings life.	Paper	Place less able students in pairs		English – present information clearly and in appropriate language
25 mins	Feedback from class. Whole class discussion and teacher-led guidance on lifecycle costing and the benefits	Students answering and asking questions, and recording information	Paper PowerPoint slides	Use prompt questions and ideas for less able students	Debate to encourage independent formation of ideas	English – improvement of skills through debate

20 mins	Discussion of benefits Observation of diagram on SB p207 used as stimulus for discussion	SB p207	Observation of benefits Discussing in groups the different benefits. Place groups according to a ability, with a range of ability in each group	Improve teamwork through group exercise	
20 mins	Introduction of tasks and information they will need for next session – investigation into the sustainable lifecycle costs associated with a new development Take note of instructions for homework, to carry out personal skills activity on p206 SB	SB p206 personal skills activity	More able students can be encouraged to investigate life cycle costing, and examples, independently	Independent enquirers – investigating lifecycle costs	IT – encourage independent research as homework
5 mins	Plenary Review of learning objectives	Q&A session to reflect on learning	How can a building have a lifecycle? What does lifecycle costing involve? Who stands to benefit from lifecycle costing?	Reflective students – consider what they have learnt to secure learning	

Lesson plan 2

Unit 7: Value and use of the built environment: Facilities management – Lifecycle costing and sustainability 2

Centre Name:

Tutor/Lecturer(s):

Aims & objectives

- To consider what the lifecycle of a building is

SB = Student Book 1

ADR = Assessment and Delivery Resource

Learning outcomes

- All students should understand what is meant by the life cycle costing and sustainable benefits to a building LO.7.2/3

Timings reflect one typical session within the GLH block of 3 hours allocated in the SOW

Total lesson time: 90 minutes

Timing/Content	Tutor activity	Student activity	Resources	Individualised activity/differentiation	Personal learning and thinking skills	Functional skills
5 mins Welcome students and register	Check health and safety of the room. Take a register	Enter room in accordance with normal procedures and settle quickly	Register			
10 mins Starter activity	Run quick-fire question feedback from homework – investigation into the sustainable lifecycle costs associated with a new development	Feed back results of personal skills activity set for homework	Paper Student's homework from earlier topic		Team workers – able to manage input from others in group and encourage discussion	

Time	Teacher activity	Student activity	Resources	Differentiation	Teamwork through partner work	English skills
15 mins	Introduce Activity 2 SB p207	Five minutes discussion with partner on Activity 2. Consider the city centre shopping complex and sustainability issues	Activities SB p207. Paper	Encourage less able students with prompt questions and ideas		English skills – debate and discussion
15 mins	Assist pairs when required	In pairs, write a response to the questions within Activity 2. Consider the sustainability issues surrounding the shopping complex	Paper, computer		Effective participators – able to discuss issues with others they may not know so well	
10 mins	Introduction to Activity 3 (SB p207) – how to write up the response like a proposal	Take notes on how to complete Activity 3 (SB p207)	Computer with internet access for further research if required	Provide writing frames for students who need them		English skills – through reporting; IT – independent Internet research
30 mins	Move around classroom to ensure that students are on task. Give praise and assistance where required	Complete Activity 3 – write a proposal to the local council to try to persuade them that this project (in Activity 2) deserves support	Computer, internet access for further research if required	Provide writing frames for students who need them		
5 mins Plenary	Review of learning objectives	Join in Q&A session to reflect on learning	How can a building have a lifecycle? What does lifecycle costing involve? Who stands to benefit from lifecycle costing?	Provide writing frames for students who need them	Reflective students – consider what they have learnt to secure learning	

7.1   Facilities management provision

Student Book
pp 196–197

1   The hospital services manager is unsure what services you have contracted out as part of the hospital's facilities policy. On the list, circle the services that would typically be contracted out.

   ■ Ward cleaning

   ■ Operating staff

   ■ Senior consultants

   ■ Waste removal

   ■ Landscape gardening

   ■ Telephone services

   ■ Ambulance services

   ■ Car parking

2   The hospital's management team is very keen on facilities management. They have asked you to consider what other services (apart from those on the above list) could be contracted out to specialist subcontractors.

   Produce a list of services that can be considered by the hospital management board.

3   The facilities manager is concerned about the performance of one of the contractors on the hospital site. They have been slow to respond to requests and have in some cases not met the agreed targets of performance. You have been asked to write a short report on what measures could be used to bring this contractor back to the agreed standard.

   Produce a list of bullet points that will act as prompts for this report.

   Undertake some research and identify what measures the facilities manager could make to monitor and correct performance.

7.2   Maintenance

Student Book
pp 198–199

1   Acting as the building company, draw up a contract on general maintenance (i.e. to put right things that go wrong), lasting for a period of 12 months, that will allow the future owner to feel satisfied when buying the property.

2   List as many defects as you can think of that could happen on a building as a result of poor build quality. For each one, explain why it might occur.

Type of defect	Reason for arising

7.3   How facilities services are provided

**Student Book
pp 200–201**

1   Your manager has asked you to help produce an advert to be placed in a construction news magazine.

Your task is to write a short job description for a facilities manager, designed to attract the correct standard of people for the position within the company. Make sure your advert includes:

■   a list of the main responsibilities

■   the sort of 'construction' skills needed

■   the sort of 'people' skills needed

2   A local developer has had planning permission rejected on a local community sports facility, because it would not contribute economically to the community.

Find such a building in your local area. Identify three potential economic factors that show how it *does* contribute to the local economy.

3   From the following list identify the materials that would last the longest when used on the exterior of a house.

■   Softwood boarding

■   Clay tiles

■   Copper sheeting panels

■   Lead flashings

■   Concrete roof tiles

■   Engineering brickwork

■   uPVC fascias

■   Timber window frames

7.4   Facilities maintenance

Student Book
pp 202–203

1   Regular maintenance of a building's services and systems is essential if the building is to run smoothly and efficiently. From the following list, identify those items that will require regular maintenance by a specialist contractor:

- windows

- lifts

- escalators

- boiler management systems

- sprinkler systems

- damp proof courses

- ventilation systems

- roof timbers

- air conditioning

- tarmac car parks

- landscaping

2   Health and safety is vital in facilities management. Imagine you are considering a bid from a window cleaning contractor to clean the windows of three storey buildings on site.

What precautions must you take to prevent accidents from falls? What measures could be taken when designing a new building to help prevent falls in the future? Write a short report.

3   Lettings are a function of facilities management. Just what are they? Do some research to find out.

Identify some local examples of lettings that provide efficient use of buildings that would otherwise close at teatime.

7.5 Planned maintenance

Student Book
pp 204–205

1   You are in charge of a local authority housing estate maintenance team. The checklist of what requires to be maintained has been left out in the rain and several of the items are missing. Fill in the missing checklist items.

2   Match each item against the appropriate maintenance technique.

Gas test	Lift inspection cover and rod
Window hinges	Switch off and replace
Electrical test	Push test button
Dripping tap	Spray with lubricant
Blocked drain	Use a Corgi-registered fitter

3   You have just joined the local authority's planned maintenance team as an assistant site supervisor. The director of maintenance has asked you to look at the current housing stock that the council owns and produce a checklist that can be used by any maintenance team to assess what needs replacing or maintaining.

Produce a checklist under the following headings by providing points in the right-hand side of the table.

General	
External	
Internal	

7.6   Sustainability: Life cycle costing

Student Book
pp 206–207

1   As a developer, you are briefing an architect to design an out-of-town retail development. Part of the architect's remit is to produce a design that takes into account the whole lifecycle of the project – but the architect calls you asking what you mean by this.

Write a reply to the architect, answering the following questions:

■ What does lifecycle refer to?

■ What is lifecycle costing?

■ What parts of the building's services would benefit from lifecycle costing?

■ What parts of the specification could use recycled materials?

■ Does the cost of the land need to be taken into account in lifecycle costing?

2   A building's energy consumption is a factor in the lifecycle costing equation. What methods could be used to reduce the energy cost of the life of a project? Make a list of at least six items.

3   You are living in a local community housing project. This consists of flats and semi-detached social housing. You have been elected onto the estate committee in order to speak on behalf of the tenants. They have complained about how small a proportion of the maintenance costs is being spent on the estate.

Given that so little is available for maintenance on this estate, identify what measures the housing association could utilise in order to reduce the cost of maintenance.

7.7   Property services

Student Book
pp 208–209

1   The management of property can be a complicated process for the manager. Fill in the following missing words that have been left out of this sentence on property management.

Property management involves the buildings sy____s, occupants and ser___s that make up the complete building. These have to be managed to r_____ wastage, obtain eff_____, and provide a pleasant and s_____ environment for its workers.

2   Use the internet to identify different types of property services available to be managed by specialists. Use your research findings to answer the following questions:

■ Do landlords feature in property management? If so, in what way?

■ Can you employ a specialist to manage your property?

■ Can the workforce be managed? If so, how?

■ What areas of your business systems could be managed?

3   You have employed the services of an estate agent to look after the portfolio of houses that you rent out to local tenants. This company undertakes this as part of their business. You have had several complaints from your tenants that, when they have terminated the rent agreement, a large part of their deposit has been withheld, although there has been no damage.

What can you do to prevent this happening?

_____

_____

_____

_____

_____

_____

_____